# Contents

Kiki in
7

Life is full of surprises
31

Competition is good for business
54

Who's the most beautiful of them all?
77

Kiki's had enough
99

Tears, training, terrific guys
124

Catwalk cows
150

Catwalk dreams
174

Love don't cost a thing
198

# Kiki in crisis

"**For crying out loud**, girl, watch out where you're going!"

As usual I'd heard the school bell late and was just rushing along the corridor when I ran into an unexpected **obstacle** in front of our classroom: a girl who I'd never seen before in our school. What was she standing around here for, **blocking** my way? **Whatever**. There was no time to find out anyway because the way things looked, the lesson had already started inside the classroom. What a pain! It was about time I sorted out my problem with **punctuality**.

I was just about to reach for the **door handle**, but the new girl got there before me. After knocking briefly, she opened the door. Then she just stood there with a big grin on her face. What was she playing at? I pushed her to one side.

"Do you mind? I don't want to **grow roots** here," I said in not my friendliest tone.

All the other kids in the class turned to look at us in

---

For crying out loud! – Mensch!; obstacle – Hindernis; to block – versperren; whatever! – egal!; punctuality – Pünktlichkeit; door handle – Türklinke; to grow roots – Wurzeln schlagen

the doorway. Our Biology teacher, Moffel, too. The new girl was still standing there. **As far as I was concerned,** she could have become a permanent **addition** to the door-frame. I just squeezed past her and **scuttled** over to my chair while mumbling an apology.

But Moffel didn't even hear me. The new girl had his **undivided attention**.

"My name's Mona," she said **confidently**. "I was told to come to this class and ask for Mr Morgentau."

Mr Morgentau! Tzzz! It sounded strange to hear her say our Biology teacher's name. I mean, we'd been calling him nothing but Moffel since Year 5. It was our affectionate **nickname** for him. After all, he was one of the really nice teachers.

I **giggled** and whispered to my friend Franzi "That's not the new girl who Wölfchen told us about, is it?"

But before Franzi could give me an answer, Moffel jumped up and said, "You must be the new pupil who Mr Wolf **entrusted to** me."

All the boys snorted with laughter and the class-macho, Fabian, **predictably** came up with a **suggestive comment** straightaway. "I wouldn't mind if she were entrusted to me!" he said with a whistle through his teeth.

For some incomprehensible reason Moffel liked Fabi-

---

as far as I was concerned – von mir aus; addition – Anbau; to scuttle – sich davonmachen; undivided attention – ungeteilte Aufmerksamkeit; confidently – selbstbewusst; nickname – Spitzname; to giggle – kichern; to entrust to sb – jmdm. ans Herz legen; predictably – erwartungsgemäß; a suggestive comment – eine anzügliche Bemerkung

an, and so he just narrowed his eyes and said, "I think she's better off with me for the time being. And by the way, without wanting to get too close to you, not every girl wants to be entrusted to you!"

**Bull's eye**! That **triggered off a volley of laughter** amongst the girls. I was just one example of the girls who'd spent weeks trying to **fob off** Fabian's pushy attempts to **come on to** me.

But that's another story.

Meanwhile Mona had come into the classroom and closed the door behind her. She seemed to be a sunshine girl because she still had a broad smile on her face. Still, you had to admit – **unbegrudgingly** if possible – that she was pretty good-looking. But the permanent smile did begin to make her look a bit stupid.

She went up to Moffel confidently and shook hands with him.

"Hallo and welcome," he said. "We're always happy to have new pupils who are nice."

"Particularly of the female **variety**!" Sebastian, who wasn't much better than Fabian, **chipped in**.

Mona gave Moffel a big smile and then she turned to the class and did the same. "Thanks a lot! I'm sure I'm really going to like it here. I've got the feeling I'm going to make friends really quickly."

The boys whistled again and Fabian called out, "No

---

bull's eye – Volltreffer; to trigger off a volley of laughter – eine Lachsalve auslösen; to fob off – abwimmeln; to come on to sb – jmdn. anbaggern; unbegrudging – neidlos; variety – Art; to chip in – dazwischenreden

problem!" He lifted up the empty chair next to him. "There's a seat free here ... and there's room for you in my heart as well!"

**Howls of laughter**.

I started to find the whole thing embarrassing. The **fuss** they were **kicking up** over the new girl! "Did you hear that? *Friends*?!" I said to Franzi, my best friend, sullenly. "She's got her eyes on our boys!"

"Oh, rubbish!" Franzi waved her hand **dismissively** without taking her eyes off Mona.

But I wasn't going to give up.

"So why did she say *friends* and not *girlfriends* then?"

"Don't you start! Everybody says *friends*."

"Well, then she's hardly emancipated in her use of language!"

For a moment Franzi turned her attention away from Moffel and the new girl. She stared at me in amazement and tapped her forehead with her finger. "Are you completely **off your rocker**!"

Meanwhile Moffel had set about the next activity and was looking for a suitable place for our new **classmate**. "So, where can we put you ...?" he said, thinking out loud.

And, of course, every single boy in the class immediately cried out, "Here!"

The new girl obviously felt deeply **flattered** because

---

howls of laughter – Gejohle; to kick up a fuss – Wirbel machen; dismissively – wegwerfend; to be off one's rocker – nicht mehr alle Tassen im Schrank haben; classmate – Klassenkamerad; flattered – geschmeichelt

her permanent smile grew even broader. Then Moffel spotted a chair. Next to Sophie. Almost within **arm's length** of me. Damn and blast! Couldn't she **enchant** somebody else with the sight of her back? I could do without her long hair blocking my view of the **board**. It was almost **indecent** how long her hair was. And I knew perfectly well that boys were **crazy about** hair like that.

"Have you got a problem with her?" asked Franzi. "You look really **on edge**."

Stupid question. Of course, I had a problem with her! I mean, I couldn't exactly say why, but the way she'd stood in the doorway back there, grinning her face off, and the way Fabian immediately started coming on to her, I just knew I was going to have stress with her.

At morning **break** the new girl was – of course – the centre of attention. It was inevitable really, but still it **stank**, above all because nearly all the boys were **flocking around** her, even the ones who weren't usually interested in girls. She must really have some **charisma**!

"Man, get your **backside** off my table!" I snapped at Sebastian as he was just about to deposit his **considerable corpulence** on it. He flattened whatever he sat upon! I quickly packed my pencil case and books into my rucksack. **Better safe than sorry**. I'd only just cleared the

---

arm's length – Armlänge; to enchant – entzücken; board – Tafel;
indecent – unanständig; to be crazy about sth –
nach etwas verrückt sein; on edge – angespannt; break – Pause;
to stink – ätzend sein; to flock around sb – sich um jmdn. scharen;
charisma – Ausstrahlung; backside – Hintern;
considerable corpulence – beachtliche Körperfülle;
Better safe than sorry – Vorsicht ist besser als Nachsicht

table when Fabian sat down on it – as if I'd just cleared it for him! But he wasn't interested in me. He only had eyes and ears for the new girl, and she was **basking in** all the attention being paid to her. All of a sudden, I found it unbearably **muggy** in the classroom.

"Do you want to catch a breath of fresh air with me?" I asked Franzi. "I could **suffocate** in here."

A **puzzled** look from her. "Do you think so?"

She didn't go to follow me. She still seemed to be **under the spell** of our new pupil, and she stayed where she was. That's how I ended up standing outside in the corridor, frustrated and alone, while everyone else was **gathered** around Mona in the classroom. It was an **unfortunate** situation.

My self-confidence was at an all-time low. I'd rarely felt so **redundant** … *I'm useless, but not for long, the future is coming on, is coming on, my future …*

But instead of a better future arriving, my second best friend, Lea, turned up. She was on her way back from the toilet, and she looked at me questioningly. "What's up? Why are you standing around here on your own?"

"I don't feel well," I said, and that wasn't so far from the truth. I could really have **spewed** at the sight of my classmates dancing around the new girl like Israelites around **the Golden Calf**.

---

to bask in sth – sich in etwas sonnen; muggy – schwül; to suffocate – ersticken; puzzled – irritiert; to be under sb's spell – unter jmds. Bann stehen; to gather – sammeln; unfortunate – misslich; redundant – überflüssig; to spew – speien; the Golden Calf – das Goldene Kalb

"It will soon **blow over**," Franzi tried to **reassure** me later. "It's just **curiosity**."

But my day had been ruined already. Everybody – including my very best friend Franzi – had spent the entire morning with eyes and ears for Mona alone. Each teacher she introduced herself to seemed to be mad about her on the spot, and even our **forbidding** English teacher, Mrs Ingrimm, almost fell over herself to be friendly.

And the only thing Franzi could say was, "Stop being so **resentful**, Kiki. She seems to be a nice person to me. You have to give her a chance."

Give her a chance! Was I Caritas or Mother Teresa?

Our class had only just managed to get a sense of togetherness. We didn't need anyone to come along and **mess** it all **up**. Especially the **shaky rapport** between the sexes. And you couldn't help seeing the effect she had on our boys. It all spelled disaster!

"Don't you think she's a bit ... a bit ...?" I tried to find the right word, but I couldn't think of it straightaway, so I just kept **chewing** the potato in my mouth. I was sitting with Franzi in the canteen, stuffing my face with food without the slightest pleasure.

"... a bit what? What are you trying to say?" Franzi looked at me annoyed.

Franzi was showing absolutely no willingness to understand me.

---

to blow over – abflauen; to reassure – beruhigen;
curiosity – Neugierde; forbidding – grimmig;
resentful – missgünstig; to mess sth up – etwas vermasseln;
shaky rapport – wackliges Verhältnis; to chew – kauen

"You know, she's just a bit ... strange. You know, a bit arrogant. She's so ... so ... **overtly** sure of herself ..."

It was difficult to describe the strange impression that Mona made on me. But the way she turned up in the classroom although she didn't know anybody there – that just wasn't normal.

"Well, in my opinion she's perfectly normal," Franzi cut short my thoughts. "She's **straightforward**, nice-looking, is obviously nice as well, and she seems to know what she wants."

"Yeah, our boys most of all!" I grumbled with my mouth full.

"Stop being so **bitchy**! You weren't interested in them at all until now!"

Franzi was exaggerating somewhat there. Just because I didn't let myself be **fooled by** every single boy, didn't mean that I wasn't interested. And I certainly wasn't just going to stand by and look on as some girl like Mona came strolling along and tried to get her **grubby** hands on our male classmates.

No, Franzi had to agree with me. She was taking this new girl far too lightly.

"Stop **dodging** the issue!" I said.

As I looked up from my plate, the next mouthful of potato almost fell off my fork. Mona had appeared from nowhere and was standing in front of our table with her

---

overtly – unverhohlen; straightforward – unkompliziert;
bitchy – zickig;
to be fooled by sb – sich von jmdm. einwickeln lassen;
grubby – schmutzig; to dodge – ausweichen

**tray**. She even asked if she could sit down with us. No way, I thought, get lost!

But Franzi gestured to Mona to take a seat, saying, "Sure, go ahead. There's plenty of room," and she pushed her tray to one side so that Mona could put hers down.

And then she really sat down next to me! My stomach turned. While Franzi started an obviously extremely **stimulating** conversation with her, I **picked listlessly** at my food. I'd completely lost my appetite.

There was nothing I wanted more right then than to go home and work off my frustration by walking my dog. But no, Mum just had to send me to this **full-time day school**! She just wanted to make sure I was "**taken care of**". She spent all her time at her **advertising agency**, and so she thought a school like this was the best place for me. Not even my non-stop **moaning** could change her mind.

"It means you can have a decent lunch and spend the afternoon with your friends in **study-groups** and doing sport. That's much better than **squatting** in front of the television at home. And it means I don't always have to cook something for you right after getting home from work when I'm feeling really tired."

This solution was particularly practical for Mum after my brother Alexander – also known as "the (Pain-)

---

tray – Tablett; stimulating – anregend;
to pick listlessly – lustlos herumstochern;
full-time day school – Ganztagsschule; taken care of – versorgt;
advertising agency – Werbeagentur;
to moan – nörgeln; study-group – Arbeitsgemeinschaft;
to squat – hocken

Joker" – started in Year 5 and came to my school. He earned his nickname with his two unusual character traits: either he made really funny jokes or he was a real **pain in the neck**.

But anyway, school wasn't all that bad. The study-groups in the afternoon were always a good laugh and – a particular **bonus** – where else did you have so much time to flirt with the boys?! Our schoolyard had a lot of green **nooks and crannies** between the buildings, providing ideal conditions for flirting, particularly when we had free lessons.

Not that I was **desperate for** a boyfriend. But constantly being **chatted up** by boys was starting to get on my nerves, and Franzi's arguments concerning this matter gradually came to make sense to me: "If you have a boyfriend," she **claimed**, "the other boys don't bother you in the schoolyard. It's as if someone had given you some anti-boy-**deodorant**."

I giggled because we always sprayed anti-dog-spray on the fence to keep away the male dogs when Sniffy was **on heat** – though the spray seemed to lose its effectiveness every time it rained.

Franzi grinned at this cutting **comparison** but said that a boyfriend had a longer **shelf life**.

---

a pain in the neck – eine Nervensäge;
bonus – Pluspunkt; nooks and crannies – Ecken und Winkel;
to be desperate for sth – etwas dringend brauchen;
to chat up – anbaggern; to claim – behaupten;
deodorant – Körperspray; to be on heat – läufig sein;
comparison – Vergleich; shelf life – Haltbarkeitsdatum

"Take Sunny, for example. She leads a completely **undisturbed** life now that she's with Tim."

She'd **convinced** me. A boyfriend in the role of personal bodyguard wasn't such a bad idea.

"OK," I said. "You try to **swing** it with Raffi and I … hum … who's going to be my **victim**? I won't take just anyone."

And there it was: my problem. And it was a problem which had remained unsolved since our conversation. I was determined to wait for Mr Right. The only problem was: it wasn't so easy deciding who he was.

I heaved a big, bellowing **sigh**, and Mona looked right at me. She had bluish green eyes. Like a big cat, I thought.

"Are you feeling alright?" she asked, and her voice rang with **sanctimonious compassion**.

How could I possibly be alright when she was robbing me of my people's attention? I nodded and made an effort to behave as normally as possible.

Pull yourself together, Kiki! cried a **benign** voice inside me.

"I'm fine," I said, trying to sound as **cheerful** as possible. "The food is just so **gross** again."

All she needed to do was agree with me, but no, she just had to **contradict** me.

---

undisturbed – ungestört; to convince – überzeugen;
to swing sth – etwas deichseln; victim – Opfer; sigh – Seufzer;
sanctimonious – scheinheilig; compassion – Mitleid;
benign – wohlmeinend; cheerful – fröhlich; gross – ekelig;
to contradict – widersprechen

"I think it's quite tasty, actually. I mean, for a school canteen it's not bad at all."

OK, now that wasn't down to me! If Mona wanted to take a course for confrontation, then she was heading the right way.

"Yeah, well, if you're not used to anything better!" I said, a touch more **harshly** than I wanted. Franzi glared at me angrily again.

Mona raised her left eyebrow slightly – creating a facial expression of exceptional arrogance in my opinion – but she then let the comment go over her head.

She carefully put her cutlery down on her plate for a moment and said in a quiet and friendly tone, "Of course, my mum cooks much better than this, but you can't **compare** home cooking with a school canteen. I mean, it's not a first class restaurant here."

First class restaurant! Not bad, the **airs** she **gave herself**. It made her sound like she always hung out in **top-notch** locations. She was just saying that to make me jealous. No, there was absolutely no point! I was quite sure now: Mona was an **opinionated**, arrogant little bitch. She couldn't fool me. And the others would all soon realise that she had her **foibles** as well.

I stood up, grabbed my tray and said brusquely to Franzi, "Are you coming?"

It sounded like an **order**. Franzi was so surprised by

---

harsh – scharf; to compare – vergleichen;
to give oneself airs – vornehm tun, sich aufspielen;
top-notch – erstklassig; opinionated – eingebildet;
foible – Macke; order – Befehl

my sudden move that she dropped her fork. It **tinkled** against her glass and then fell onto her tray. She stared at her plate – which was still half full – then at me. Her face was a picture of the conflict going on inside her: should she show her solidarity to me or continue to satisfy her lunchtime hunger? The hunger won.

"You go ahead," she said guiltily. "I'll just quickly finish eating."

Did I see a **smirk** of satisfaction on Mona's face?

What a blow! Now I'd have to stand around in the schoolyard on my own while that silly cow took her time over lunch with my best friend! I hated that day!

"Oh dear! All on your own and feeling lonely?" said someone at my side. It was Fabian. Why wasn't he hanging around the new girl with his clique?

"Already lost interest in Mona?" I asked **on the spur of the moment** – which was, of course, tactically very **unwise** of me. I immediately **got my just deserts** for my indiscreet comment.

"Jealous?"

Not that again! Did everybody around here **have a screw loose**? I just managed to catch myself.

"Have you got any more jokes like that **up your sleeve**?"

---

to tinkle – klirren; smirk – Grinsen;
on the spur of the moment – spontan; unwise – unklug;
to get one's just deserts – seine Quittung bekommen;
to have a screw loose – einen Schraube locker haben;
to have sth up one's sleeve – etwas auf Lager haben

He gave a cheeky laugh. "Sure I have!"

Thank God I didn't have to listen to them because Sebastian and the rest of the boys' gang came **strolling** out of the canteen into schoolyard and Fabian immediately went running over to them.

Where had Franzi got to? The Art study-group was about to start and I didn't want to be late.

Art was by far my favourite study-group. I was really good at it. I must have **inherited** some talent from my mum. She worked for an advertising agency as a graphic designer. On top of that, the Art study-group teacher, van Gogh, was my favourite teacher. He was Dutch, and his real name was van Linde, but since the **memorable** day when he said to Fabian, "Don't shout like that in my ear – otherwise it will fall off!" we decided to give him a nickname. We'd just spent weeks studying the work of the painter, van Gogh, and we couldn't help thinking of his self-portrait after he'd cut off his ear.

"I'm **honoured**," van Gogh had said with his slight accent and a smile as he learned of this. "After all, van Gogh was Dutch, too."

Eventually, Franzi turned up in the schoolyard – with that awful Mona **in tow**, of course. Hopefully, she didn't want to join the Art study-group as well?! But she did – which I thought was really **mean** of her. Why didn't she take Music with **Twitterbird**?

---

to stroll – schlendern; to inherit – erben;
memorable – denkwürdig; to honour – ehren;
in tow – im Schlepptau; mean – gemein, fies;
twitterbird – Zwitscherschwalbe

"Wouldn't you rather take Music?" I quickly tried to **convert** her. "The Art study-group is pretty full and dead boring. Really, spare yourself the pain."

Franzi looked at me in amazement and was completely **at a loss**. "And I always thought Art was your favourite study-group," she said **gullibly**.

**Blimey!** The girl was **slow on the uptake**! She'd made me look ridiculous!

"Hm, yeah," I tried to rescue the situation. "At the beginning it was, but now it's really **mind-numbing**."

Franzi's eyes opened even wider. I ought to be careful they didn't pop out of her head when I next spoke.

Mona looked from me to Franzi and then back to me with a puzzled expression on her face. "That sounds terrible," she said. "But I'm a complete **loser** in Music. I don't have a choice. I'll have to share your **fate** with you and join the Art study-group, no matter how boring it is."

Damn, that didn't work at all! I tried to hide my annoyance at my failed **counter-attack** by grabbing Franzi by the arm and pulling her away from Mona.

"Then we'll meet you there. It's in art room number 2, on the first floor. We have to go to our **lockers** first."

---

to convert sb – jmdn. umpolen;
to be at a loss – nicht durchblicken; gullibly – leichtgläubig, einfältig; Blimey! – Verflucht!;
to be slow on the uptake – schwer von Begriff sein;
mind-numbing – langweilig; loser – Niete; fate – Schicksal;
counter-attack – Gegenangriff; locker – Schließfach

We'd only just got out of Mona's sight when I **had a** real **go at** Franzi. "Are you off your rocker? Why are you **dragging** her along to the Art study-group?"

"Me? Why me? It's not my **fault** she's interested in Art," said Franzi. She sounded really **infuriated**. "I can't stop anyone from choosing the study-groups they like."

"Don't get so **worked up**," I tried to calm her down. "But the idea of having to put up with that girl this afternoon as well is really unbearable."

For some reason Franzi had a completely different point of view from me, and there was nothing I could do to persuade her otherwise.

"I think you're being real bitchy for no real reason. Just wait and see what she's like."

I could already see what she was like. I didn't need to wait and see. She was a real **bootlicker**! And the worst thing was that even my best friend didn't notice it.

**Needless to say**, the Art study-group was ruined for me.

Especially when Mona **sucked up** to van Gogh with her broad, beaming smile and he **melted** in an instant.

I wanted to call out: hey, I'm your favourite pupil!

Of course, she had neither brushes nor a **sketchpad** with her, and so van Gogh had to go with her to the **store-**

---

to have a go at sb – jmdn. anfauchen; to drag – schleppen;
fault – Schuld; infuriated – zornig; worked up – aufgebracht;
bootlicker – Stiefellecker, Schleimer;
needless to say – selbstverständlich; to suck up – anschleimen;
to melt – schmelzen; sketchpad – Skizzenblock;
storeroom – Lagerraum

**room** and organise the **necessities** for her. When I heard them both laughing, I got even angrier. What was taking them so long?

They eventually came back. Mona was carrying some sketching paper, a paint box and a handful of brushes, while van Gogh followed her with a glass of water. She must have really **wrapped** him around her little finger.

Feeling furious I dabbed my brush into the red paint and slapped a thick **splodge** of it onto my picture. Hum, that was a bit **brash**! Van Gogh thought so as well. After he'd explained the task to Mona and was taking a look around the room, he turned to me with a shake of his head.

"Don't you think you've gone for the wrong colour there?" he asked.

I **refrained** from saying anything, just in case I went for the wrong tone as well.

On the way home Franzi **bore the brunt of** my anger again.

"You have to admit she really sucked up to van Gogh. She completely wrapped him around her little finger," I **let off steam**.

But Franzi is an honest sort and an absolute realist, and all she could say was, "Oh, come on! He only gave her a few materials so she could complete the task. What's wrong with that?"

---

necessity – das Nötigste; to wrap – wickeln; splodge – Klecks;
brash – schrill; to refrain – sich zurückhalten;
to bear the brunt of sth – etwas zu spüren bekommen;
to let off steam – Dampf ablassen

I spared her my answer and we sat in the **tram** in silence. When I got out, I muttered a **feeble** "see you" and traipsed home **grumpily**.

What was the point of having a best friend if she kept **stabbing you in the back**?! One can't go around **sticking up for** just anybody the way Franzi was. She'd soon find out what it brought her in the end! Nothing!

At home I grabbed the **dog's lead** and went for a run through the municipal park with Sniffy, my beloved **mongrel**. At the **pond** I did a few stretching exercises. All that **oxygen** I was breathing in helped me to start thinking more positively again, and I began to feel that familiar sense of euphoria. They say it has something to do with biological-dynamic processes which take place in the body while running. Well, it was all the same to me. Perhaps that's why I liked running off my frustration.

With my dog jumping up alongside me, **barking** happily, I also started to feel happier again.

I'd **get on top of** that Mona girl one way or another.

Maybe Franzi was right and she really wasn't so bad. Anyway, I had good friends, and when Mona's **novelty factor** wore off, no one would pay her any attention anymore. The best thing to do was wait and drink tea. And

---

tram – Straßenbahn; feeble – lasch; grumpily – grantig;
to stab sb in the back – jmdm. in den Rücken fallen;
to stick up for sb – sich für jmdn. einsetzen;
dog's lead – Hundeleine; mongrel – Promenadenmischung;
pond – Teich; oxygen – Sauerstoff; to bark – bellen;
to get on top of – in den Griff bekommen;
novelty factor – Neuigkeitswert

that's exactly what I did after having given both me and Sniffy a good shower.

I **snuggled up** in the big armchair, which my grandad had left me, and sipped at my blackberry tea while listening to a CD and enjoying the vanilla scent of the **joss sticks** burning around me. On days like this – when things didn't go well in school or anywhere else for that matter – I liked to **spoil** myself a bit at home.

I'd learned that from Mum. "Never bring stress from work home with you!" was her motto. "Your private life is there to take a break from stress. People need an island of peace and quiet if they want to **cope** with the challenges of daily life. They need to spoil themselves a bit."

And she stuck to this philosophy, especially after Dad took a job at the **Lower House of Parliament** in Berlin and she went back to work.

There were times when I would have liked to have had her **calmness**, particularly in school. But I was either lacking a few key biological **prerequisites** – for example, a **gland** to **discharge** bootlicking slime – or I really was – as our form teacher, Dr. Wolf, put it – of a "somewhat unbalanced temperament".

Mum tried to reassure me that it was better to have an unbalanced temperament than no temperament at all, but sometimes I **envied** bootlickers, like my fellow

---

to snuggle up – kuscheln; joss stick – Räucherstäbchen;
to spoil – verwöhnen; to cope – zurechtkommen;
Lower House of Parliament – Bundestag; calmness – Gemütsruhe;
prerequisite – Voraussetzung; gland – Drüse;
to discharge – absondern; to envy – beneiden

pupil, Gracia, for her easy-going, if somewhat dull life. Just the thought of that calmness, that obvious tranquillity! At the moment the smallest things could get on my nerves and I could suddenly explode with no prior warning. Stay cool, girl, stay cool! I usually tried to calm myself down because most of the time I could sense the **havoc** that my behaviour would **wreak**. But it was all **in vain**. There was nothing I could do about my nature. And on top of all that I seemed to be a magnet for chaos, embarrassing situations and misunderstandings. I was like a **light bulb** in a room full of **moths**!

Why – of all the classes in the world – did Mona have to walk into mine? Needless to say, I couldn't get her out of my head for the rest of the day, and not even my meditative exercises or mental training could drive her out. "I'm calm. I feel good. I'm free of **worries** ..."

Rubbish! All the worries of the world were **towering up** in front of me and they certainly weren't going to disappear just because of some **pan-pipe** music coming out of the CD player!

But as I drank my second cup of tea and stroked Sniffy, who I'd just **blow-dried**, on my lap, the situation didn't seem to be quite so hopeless to me. After all, I wasn't exactly ugly myself, and there were even guys out there who thought my blonde hair was great. Even if it was just **sweet-talking** most of the time, there was hardly anyone

---

to wreak havoc – schlimme Schäden anrichten;
in vain – vergeblich; light bulb – Glühbirne; moth – Motte;
worry – Sorge; to tower up – sich türmen; pan-pipe – Panflöte;
to blow-dry – föhnen; sweet-talking – Süßholzgeraspel

else who was such a natural blonde as me. I sighed **with relief** at the thought. The boys would go back to normal and everything would take its usual path.

Besides, it was the "**Women's Lib meeting**" in the first lesson the next day. That was the name the boys had given to our girls' group, the *Pepper Dollies*, which Franzi, Lea, Greetje – our Art teacher's daughter – and I had founded. Greetje came up with the name because "doll" means something like "crazy" or "unconventional" in Dutch. That **suited** us perfectly because we saw ourselves as a **counter-movement** to the bootlickers and wanted to **spice up** the school with a bit of pepper – or even some red hot chilli! – and ... well, you know ... make the boys a bit hot as well. Above all we wanted to do lots of **wacky** and crazy things! Fun was the magic word. Otherwise life was just dead boring!

After we'd set up our group, the boys inevitably thought they had to be mega-cool and match us. When, in the main break, Fabian proudly announced that the boys had set up a "gang", we almost laughed our heads off.

"A gang!!" Lea snorted with laughter.

"You couldn't have started smaller by any chance!" **scoffed** Franzi.

"And what have you **christened** yourselves?" asked Greetje with her cute Dutch accent. "Dolly Dumbos?"

---

with relief – erleichtert; Women's Lib meeting – Emanzentreff;
to suit – passen; counter-movement – Gegenbewegung;
to spice up – aufpeppen; wacky – schräg; to scoff – spotten;
to christen – taufen

We roared with laughter. "Dolly Dumbos" was really great and it **suited them to a T**!

It's a well-known fact that the male sex often lacks in humour during puberty. This is because they're constantly in danger of **drowning** in their own importance. Fabian and his men were deeply insulted and they left us alone. We only managed to find out the name of the "gang" **the roundabout way** – by **bribing** Snorkel with a packet of cigarettes. We could have guessed. It had to be hip, and hop, and rappy, and futuristic, and really breathtaking. The only thing that filled us with **awe** was how stupid it was: "*Gorillas*!" Lea told us of her findings. "They've called themselves *the Gorillas*."

"They're just **making a monkey out of us**!" giggled Franzi.

I tried to imagine our male classmates as primates. The only one who could possibly pass as anything close to a gorilla was Fabian – and maybe Sebastian, too. It was more difficult to imagine Mutz in the role, and the thought of Raffi as an orang-utan was beyond my powers of imagination. He was a really small guy who was as **cuddly** as a teddy bear! I laughed as I **recalled** these memories. While nibbling at a biscuit, I hummed the latest *Gorillaz* hit: "*... There's a monkey in the jungle ...*"

My mobile phone rang. Franzi.

---

to suit to a T – haargenau passen; to drown – ertrinken;
the roundabout way – auf Umwegen; to bribe – bestechen;
awe – Ehrfurcht, Bewunderung;
to make a monkey out of sb – jmdn. zum Affen machen;
cuddly – knuddelig; to recall – sich an etwas erinnern

"Well? Have you calmed down now?"

I had, but if she talked to me like that she'd soon **get my back up** again. However, I managed to restrain myself and said with categorical **casualness**, "I never really get worked up. Just imagine what would happen if I did? So, what's up?"

"Lea wants to know if the meeting is going ahead in the free lesson tomorrow and whether we should invite Mona."

I felt like someone was waving a red flag in front of my nose. Were they trying to **provoke** me?

But this time I was much more **skilful** in my response. "What do you think?" I asked.

Franzi **hummed and hawed**.

"Yeah, well, I mean, why not?" she said in the end. "After all, she's a girl."

"But not every girl in the class is in the *Pepper Dollies*!" I tried to sound as **objective** as possible.

"That's true," Franzi had to admit.

"And maybe it wouldn't be the right thing for her," I tried to **undermine** Franzi's opinion. "I mean, you wouldn't become a member of any old thing – a political party or a gardening club – if you were new in a town, would you? You'd need some time to **get your bearings** first and then you'd be able to decide for yourself."

---

to get sb's back up – jmdn. in Rage bringen;
casualness – Gelassenheit; to provoke – provozieren;
skilful – geschickt; to hum and haw – herumdrucksen;
objective – sachlich; to undermine – untergraben;
to get one's bearings – sich orientieren

Franzi had no choice but to agree.

"You see! Then let Mona get her bearings first. She needs to get to know the others in class as well. Maybe she suits the bootlickers better."

I should have left that last comment because it just **triggered off** Franzi's opposition again: "Well, I don't think she'd get on with them. She's far too straightforward."

Oh no, I thought, she's really let Mona wrap her around her little finger! On the other hand, most people didn't like the bootlickers in the class – Gracia, Lydia and Daphne. But it was their own fault. They were completely uncool. They never had their own opinion, always said whatever the teacher wanted, never forgot their homework and they even cleaned the blackboard and carried the tests for the teacher into the **staffroom** to get a good mark.

The new girl really wasn't that **mousy** and **square**. On the contrary … that was the problem. She seemed to be a lively character, and she behaved so as well! The clothes she wore alone. And the way she carried herself. Really stylish and easy-going. I sighed.

"OK," I **met** Franzi **halfway**. "We can talk it over tomorrow and, if need be, we can **take a vote** on it."

That was a **genuinely** democratic offer.

Tomorrow there'd still be time to make a **fiery speech** against taking Mona into the *Pepper Dollies*, but I didn't mention that to Franzi right now.

---

to trigger off – auslösen; staffroom – Lehrerzimmer; mousy – farblos; square – streberhaft; to meet sb halfway – jmdm. entgegenkommen; to take a vote – abstimmen; genuinely – wirklich; fiery speech – flammende Rede

## Life is full of surprises

I couldn't sleep at all that night. I fell into the thick splodge of red paint in my picture from the Art study-group and wandered through a wild landscape of colour which was like a huge, **insane maze**. I woke up at around 3 o'clock in the morning, **drenched** in sweat. I couldn't go back to sleep, so until the alarm clock rang, I spent the time **drafting** numerous versions of a fiery speech to convince my friends that they shouldn't take Mona into our club.

I could have spared myself the effort.

First of all, I lost the vote, and secondly, Mona turned down the offer with thanks just before our English lesson after Lea had told her the good news.

"That's really very kind of you," she said with a meaningful look to me and Franzi. "But I hope you understand: I don't want to **commit** myself to any particular group until I've settled in. Maybe later."

Bang! That was a **slap** in the face. Franzi was really **shaken**.

---

insane – verrückt; maze – Labyrinth;
drenched – völlig durchnässt; to draft – entwerfen;
to commit – sich binden, festlegen; slap – Ohrfeige;
shaken – erschüttert

"And I **put my neck on the line** for her," she whispered to me in the English lesson all worked up – only to end up getting a **special task** from our **strict** English teacher, Mrs Ingrimm.

I have to admit, I didn't have much sympathy for her. I just hoped that she'd now **got over** her Mona-mania.

The others felt the same as her.

When Mona didn't sit down next to us at lunch in the canteen – but instead sat down at an empty table next to the *Gorillas* who immediately started putting on a big show – it was **the last straw**. First the **snub**, now this act of provocation! Mona would **regret** this! She'd certainly ruined her chances with us.

It was a bit mean of me really, but I just couldn't help it: I was quite happy with the way things were developing. This is why I was whistling to myself under the shower after the **PE** study-group as Mona happened to turn on the shower next to me. She poured buckets of shower gel over herself – which smelt really good – and, as I **furtively** glanced over to her, I noticed that it was a pretty expensive **brand**. She rubbed the shower gel generously into her hair and over her body, sighing gently with pleasure at the same time. The **foam** ran thickly down her back. Mona was attractive even when she was

---

to put one's neck on the line – sich aus dem Fenster lehnen;
special task – Sonderaufgabe; strict – streng;
to get over sth – über etwas hinwegkommen;
to be the last straw – das Fass zum Überlaufen bringen;
snub – Abfuhr; to regret – bereuen;
PE (physical education) – Sport; furtively – verstohlen;
brand – Marke; foam – Schaum

naked. She was slim and her silky brown skin glistened under the water and only had a few **moles**.

I looked at the mole on my stomach. No one usually saw it because it was underneath my bikini line, but all of a sudden it started to **bother** me a bit.

It was just then – as I was staring at my mole with a deep sense of **dissatisfaction** – that Mona turned to me under the shower.

She looked at me for a moment without saying anything. Then she held out her shower gel to me.

"Do you want to try it? I think it's great. I don't use anything else. You can use it for your hair, too."

I hesitated briefly – just the thought of that delicious foam on my skin! – but then I heroically turned down her offer. No one could buy Kiki. "No, thanks!" I said. "I'm not into sweet **fragrances**!"

"Oh well, whatever you say!" For the first time Mona's voice sounded slightly **uptight**. She withdrew her hand and the shower gel, adding **tersely**, "Boys just love it!"

"And then she said, 'Boys just love it'!"

I was hanging around at the **drinks dispenser** in front of the **gym**, telling the *Pepper Dollies* about the conversation with Mona with the utmost pleasure.

"She made it **crystal-clear** she's only interested in our

---

mole – Muttermal, Leberfleck; to bother sb – jmdn. stören;
dissatisfaction – Unzufriedenheit; fragrance – Duft;
uptight – genervt; tersely – spitz;
drinks dispenser – Getränkeautomat; gym – Turnhalle;
crystal-clear – sonnenklar

boys. And the way she just sat down next to them at the table today!"

"She obviously needs people to **admire** her!"

"She's welcome to them all," said Franzi, "as long as she keeps her hands off Raffi."

I couldn't exactly understand what Franzi saw in little Raffi with his bright red ears, but if she wanted him, she could have him. I wasn't interested in him at all.

The boys in my class were generally too **silly**. They just couldn't **handle** puberty, and they either played the little macho or turned completely shy and sensitive all of a sudden. And whatever you did, you couldn't help keep **treading on** these **oddballs' toes**.

There was no question about it: boys had a tough time becoming men! This went for the *Gorillas* in particular. They were making a monkey out of themselves, the way they all ran after Mona. Even Fabian – who always played Mr Cool – was literally eating his bananas out of her hand.

But you had to **hand it to her**: she really knew how to make the best of herself. Today as well she was wearing an outfit of more than just funky clothes – the perfect mix of trendy first- and second-hand.

"You've got a real great **kit** on today!" grunted Fabian, **wolf-whistling** with his fellow **apes**.

---

to admire – bewundern; silly – albern;
to handle sth – mit etwas umgehen; oddball – Verrückte;
to tread on sb's toes – jmdm. zu nahe treten;
you've got to hand it to her – das muss man ihr lassen;
kit – (ugs.) Klamotten; to wolf-whistle – lüstern pfeifen;
ape – Affe

I sighed. The world was so unfair. We'd spent more than two years trying to teach our male classmates how to **behave** in a civilized society – but it was all in vain. And now Mona had come along and our boys had turned into **goody-goodies**! Diabolical!

"Maybe she's a witch," Lea speculated in the face of this unbelievable **transformation**, "and she's put a spell on the boys with her magical powers."

Now it was my turn to burst into laughter! I wouldn't **put anything past** Mona, but **witchcraft** – that was just ridiculous.

Lea looked at me and then walked off feeling **affronted**.

"Now I've gone and upset her," I said with a **guilty conscience**. "But she takes all that esoteric stuff far too seriously. No one in their right mind can believe in witches these days!"

At least Franzi agreed with me. "Mona's like a siren. Really very **cunning**. It's not just her good looks. Perhaps we should try and learn from her a bit."

I stared at Franzi. Excuse me? Did I just hear right? She couldn't be serious. "What do you want me to do – make a fool of myself like her?"

"Does she make a fool of herself?"

"Hadn't you noticed?"

---

to behave – sich benehmen; goody-goody – Musterknabe;
transformation – Verwandlung;
I wouldn't put anything past her – Ich traue ihr alles Mögliche zu;
witchcraft – Hexerei; affronted – beleidigt;
guilty conscience – schlechtes Gewissen; cunning – raffiniert

"The boys are making a fool of themselves, the way they all **fell for** her straightaway."

"I'd really like to know what they see in her!"

I risked it.

In the main break I talked to Fabian about his strange **behaviour**. After all, until Mona turned up, he'd been coming on to me pretty strong and that gave me a right to find out why she'd now **outstripped** me.

But Fabian just explained everything with the fact that he was **class rep**. "It's logical that I help her out a bit, settling into the class and the **lesson stuff**."

"And that's why you spend every free minute of your time hanging around her with the *Gorillas*?"

He looked at me **in amazement** and raised his eyebrows. "Does it bother you?" he asked with a **shifty** smile at the corner of his eyes. "I didn't know you were so interested in what we did in our free time!"

That's because I wasn't. I mean, Fabian was the kind of guy who a girl like me just wasn't interested in. Why should she be?

"But before Mona came along, you were coming on to Kiki the whole time!" said Franzi on the spur of the moment.

Oh no, how embarrassing! Fabian would think I was jealous of Mona because I missed being chatted up by him!

---

to fall for sb – auf jmdn. abfahren; behaviour – Verhalten;
to outstrip sb – jmdm. den Rang ablaufen;
class rep – Klassensprecher; lesson stuff – Unterrichtsstoff;
in amazement – erstaunt; shifty – hinterlistig

The way I felt must have been written all over my face because Fabian just smiled at me **condescendingly** and said, "You have to do something to fill the time, and it's pretty good fun with Mona. It could have been you instead, but I never thought you **fancied** me. Maybe I was wrong?"

I could have **strangled** him! The **conceited** idiot!

"No, you weren't wrong!" I barked at him furiously, grabbed Franzi's arm and pulled her away with me.

"Come on, let's go. Before I go for his throat," I said **irately**. "He could have saved his stupid comments and just helped me out with my homework." I could have done with some **private tuition** in Maths, for example. At least as much as Mona! Grrr!

Talking of Maths!

I had a class test coming up that day. Instead of constantly thinking about Mona and the boys, I had to deal with that and quickly pick up some of the facts.

"I need to find Greetje and clear up a few things to do with the Maths test," I said to Franzi. "I didn't understand everything."

"You're well prepared!" said Franzi a bit **grouchily**. I'd dragged her away from Fabian just as Raffi had turned up.

"You want to start something with him, right?" I asked in the most undiplomatic way.

---

condescendingly – überlegen; to fancy sb – auf jmdn. stehen; to strangle – erwürgen; conceited – eingebildet; irately – wütend; private tuition – Nachhilfe; grouchy – vermuffelt

She closed up straightaway, of course. "With who?"

"You know who! With Raffi! You should have seen yourself … completely **goggle-eyed**." Oh my giddy aunt, had I completely lost it? How could I say something like that to my best friend? Even if it was the truth … Needless to say, I soon got my just deserts.

"And, of course, you didn't make a fool of yourself with Fabian at all!" And imitating my voice in an **exaggerated** manner, she said, "Why do you spend every free minute hanging around Mona …?"

I hadn't actually said that, but I could understand that she was annoyed. But before I could apologise, she turned around and disappeared into the **commotion** of the schoolyard with her head held high.

I had no other choice than to write her a note during the Maths test in which I asked her to forgive me.

I had just finished writing the note and was **discreetly** trying to arrange for it to arrive at Franzi's desk when the **piercing** voice of our Maths teacher broke the hushed silence. "Kristina! Come to the front straightaway. Bring your test and that note with you! I'm going to give you a 6 for **cheating**!"

"B-b-but I wasn't trying to cheese … er to cheat … er … well … I didn't mean to … at all. I wasn't cheating at all!" I stuttered in shock.

All my classmates looked up from their **exercise**

---

goggle-eyes – Kulleraugen; exaggerated – übertrieben;
commotion – Getümmel; discreetly – unauffällig;
piercing – durchdringend; to cheat – mogeln;
exercise book – Heft

**books** and stared at me. Their gaze burnt like **laser beams**. My head felt like it was about to explode and I expect I turned bright red. How embarrassing.

"Come here," Logel showed no sign of **mercy**. "If you have something to say to me, you can do it in the corridor so you don't disturb the others." He stood up and strode over to my desk in three big steps. He took my exercise book in one hand and held out the other to me invitingly. "Where's the note?"

I put it in the palm of his hand and then sat there **as if** I were **paralysed**.

"Would you mind standing up?" His voice still sounded irate.

All in all he was a nice teacher – a bit **odd** but nice. He was called Logel because he always said "that's logical" at every opportunity. Unfortunately, he was **merciless** when it came to cheating. I'd really **landed myself in it**. I stood up as if I were in a trance and followed him to the door. He opened it for me.

"**Woe betide** anyone who **takes advantage of** the situation to copy each other!" he said **ominously** to the class and pushed me out into the corridor. "And now to you ..."

I finally had the chance to say something. "I really wasn't cheating. I – I just wrote a letter to say sorry ... to Franzi ... You – You can read it if you want ..."

---

laser beams – Laserstrahlen; mercy – Gnade; paralysed – betäubt;
odd – kauzig; merciless – gnadenlos;
to land oneself in it – sich etwas Schönes einbrocken;
woe betide – wehe; to take advantage of sth – etwas ausnutzen;
ominously – bedrohlich

He looked at me sceptically, but because he actually liked me and he wasn't one of the teachers who always thought the worst of their pupils, but favoured the principle of "innocent until **proved** guilty", he unfolded the letter and read what I had written to Franzi.

*Please don't be angry! I'll* ***make it up to*** *you. Shall I arrange a date for you with Raffi?*

That was embarrassing enough, but still better than being falsely **accused** of cheating.

"I see, I see," said Logel, and he couldn't help smiling to himself. "A date for Franzi with Raffi … And how do you **intend** to arrange that?"

He made no attempt to **whisper**, and I could only hope that everyone was so busy with their tests that they hadn't heard it through the slightly open door, otherwise I wouldn't have just completely **disgraced** myself, but Franzi as well.

His question was, thank God, purely rhetorical because he then folded the note up again and gave it back to me. "Put it away. You can give it to Franzi at break. I can't tolerate **surreptitious** communication like this in class. Especially not during a test." He gave me my exercise book back. "Continue with the test, and at the end of the lesson come to me for a special task. And that's the end of the matter."

---

to prove – beweisen;
to make it up to sb – etwas wieder gutmachen;
to accuse – bezichtigen; to intend – beabsichtigen;
to whisper – flüstern; to disgrace – blamieren;
surreptitious – heimlich

I took my exercise book and quickly went back into the classroom. **Phew**, I was lucky there.

If I'd have been caught by Mrs Ingrimm, then she would definitely have written my name down in the **register**. Logel really was a nice guy.

Franzi and I sat **reconciled** on a school bench. Lunch break was over and we were checking out the passing boys.

"He's for you," I said. "I mean, if things don't work out with Raffi, then he could come into question for you."

When she agreed with my opinion, she **traced** a cross in the sand with her foot. We'd been playing this game for a while, and it had never lost its **appeal**. When break was over, we would count how many crosses there were. Unfortunately, since we'd been playing it, the number of crosses grew fewer and fewer. I stood up and rubbed away today's checklist with the **sole** of my foot. I couldn't help sighing: the **selection** was getting smaller all the time.

"We're obviously getting **choosier**," I said, "or the boys in this school are just plain **average**. There's not a dream boy amongst them ..."

A noise like a **tower block** being knocked down startled me out of my thoughts. I looked up from the ground and stared into the face of a boy who looked ex-

---

phew – puh; register – Klassenbuch;
reconciled – versöhnt; to trace – zeichnen; appeal – Reiz;
sole – Sohle; selection – Auswahl; choosy – wählerisch;
average – Durchschnitt; tower block – Hochhaus

actly the **opposite** of plain average. I swallowed the rest of my **disgruntled** comments and **took a gasp of breath**. **Crikey**, where did he come from so suddenly? And where had Franzi got to …?

"Excuse me," said the guy, sounding a bit stressed, "I just have to put them down – otherwise I'm going to drop them." He dropped the towering **stack** of books he was carrying onto the bench. Then he sat down next to me and sighed. Franzi **reappeared** behind the bench. The boy with the stack of books had just blocked my view of her for a few seconds. I stared at the guy fascinated – as if he was a **supernatural apparition**. Fortunately, I found my voice again.

"What are you doing with all those books?" I asked.

"I have to bring them back to the library. It's the **class set** of the last book we read in English. I'm class rep for 9c – a pretty **humble** job. You're a **dogsbody** for everybody!"

Franzi took a book and flicked through it. "It's really long!" she said. "Are we going to have to read it as well?"

"If you get Mrs Ingrimm for English, for sure." The guy laughed. "But it looks worse than it is. Actually, it was a really exciting story."

---

opposite – Gegenteil; disgruntled – unzufrieden;
to take a gasp of breath – nach Luft ringen;
Crikey! – Meine Güte!; stack – Stapel;
to reappear – wieder auftauchen;
supernatural apparition – übersinnliche Erscheinung;
class set – Klassensatz; humble – bescheiden;
dogsbody – Handlanger

He started **piling up** the books again.

I just kept staring at this eighth Wonder of the World.

I couldn't understand why I hadn't noticed him before. On my checklist he wouldn't have just got a **tick**, he'd have got a huge **exclamation mark**! What a bit of luck that his energy **deserted** him just as he was at our bench.

I found my own reaction at least as astonishing as him.

With other guys in a similar situation I would have **broken out into a sweat**. My pulse would be going up and down like a **yo-yo**. And every thought that came into my head would be lost before I managed to bring it past my lips. But this time I didn't **stammer** and my hands weren't **moist** either when I picked up some of the books and **boldly** said, "Come on, I'll give you a hand. Otherwise you'll drop them. I'm going in the same direction."

With the books in my hand I headed towards the main building where the school library was located, leaving behind a completely **flabbergasted** Franzi. I was sorry about that, but I'd make it up to her later. I couldn't just let this boy disappear with his books. My inner voice told to me to **stick to his heels**.

"Isn't he **gorgeous**?" I whispered to Franzi at the beginning of the English lesson.

---

to pile up – stapeln; tick – Strich;
exclamation mark – Ausrufezeichen; to desert – verlassen;
to break out into a sweat – in Schweiß ausbrechen;
yo-yo – Jo-Jo; to stammer – stottern; moist – feucht;
boldly – kühn; flabbergasted – verdattert;
to stick to sb's heels – an jmdm. dranbleiben;
gorgeous – umwerfend

She still seemed **baffled** about what she'd just seen me do. After all, I was usually much more **reserved** with boys.

I'd just managed to slip into classroom before Mrs Ingrimm, and there'd only been enough time for three short sentences to explain. Mrs Ingrimm was **exceptionally** strict and didn't tolerate people talking in her class at all. She'd even spotted that I'd just whispered something to Franzi.

"Kristina, have you got something to **contribute** to the lesson? If not, stop talking."

I looked at Franzi and shrugged my shoulders in **regret**. That was my way of saying: Sorry, more later!

Needless to say, Franzi was bursting with curiosity and was pretty frustrated because she now had to wait another forty minutes for further information. It was therefore no surprise that she soon sent me a note.

*You look like you're* ***in seventh heaven****! What did you get up to in the library?*

I **hesitated**. Should I write back? I glanced across at Mrs Ingrimm who was just writing something on the blackboard, crunching the **chalk** to pieces in the process. Her **consumption** of chalk was the **caretaker**'s nightmare, and we always hid the chalk before her lessons. But

---

baffled – verblüfft; reserved – zurückhaltend;
exceptionally – außerordentlich; to contribute – beitragen;
regret – Bedauern;
to be in seventh heaven – im siebten Himmel sein;
to hesitate – zögern; chalk – Kreide; consumption – Verbrauch;
caretaker – Hausmeister

one of the bootlickers had got her another piece to **obliterate**. Oh well, let her obliterate.

I decided it would be better not to answer Franzi straightaway. I didn't want to get caught for a second time in one day, especially not by Miss-stress Ingrimm. She wasn't as **charitable** as Logel. So I whispered over to Franzi: "Later!"

But Mrs Ingrimm had long ears and a sharp tongue between them. "Exactly, Kristina! You can come and get a special task from me *later*! I warned you."

Marvellous! That was the second special task of the day. I knew what I'd be doing for the rest of the day after the end of school.

"Couldn't you have just waited until after English?" I grumbled to Franzi on our way home. But because she was genuinely sorry, I told her in the end about what had happened with me and the guy in the library.

The library block was the oldest part of our school and it had something quite **mysterious** about it. The **aisles** between the bookcases were really narrow, and the whole place was bathed in a **gloomy** light. There was something really exciting about being there alone with this dream boy, putting the books back in their place. My heart was already pounding when he turned to me and said, "Can I **return the favour** and invite you for a Coke at break tomorrow?"

---

to obliterate – vernichten; charitable – großzügig;
mysterious – geheimnisvoll; aisle – Gang; gloomy – düster;
to return a favour – sich revanchieren

I felt like something had just picked me up off the ground and I was **hovering** a few centimetres in the air. But I had **both feet** enough **on the ground** to accept straightaway.

"OK then, let's meet in the main break at the drinks dispenser in front of the gym!"

We were just going to leave the library when he suddenly disappeared behind a bookcase without saying a word.

I waited a moment, but he was nowhere to be seen. "Hello?" I called out **timidly** – after all, you're not allowed to shout in a library.

But there was no answer.

Where had he got to? Was he looking for a book to take with him?

I took a few paces back and looked down the aisle where he'd disappeared. Nothing. Had he just **legged it** without saying anything? No, I thought, that just wasn't possible: the library only had one door, and I'd been standing in front of it the whole time.

"Hello!" I called again, this time a little bit louder. "Hey! Hello? Where are you?" If only he'd told me his name! I felt stupid just saying "hey" and "hello".

Then came a funny sound: a **layman** in **ornithology** might have taken it to be the cry of an **owl**. How **droll**!

---

to hover – schweben;
to have both feet on the ground – mit beiden Beinen fest auf der Erde stehen; timidly – zaghaft; to leg it – abhauen; layman – Laie; ornithology – Vogelkunde; [tawny] owl – Käuzchen;
droll – drollig, komisch

I looked down the next aisle. Was the guy trying to **play hide and seek** with me? Then came that strange bird's call again. It wasn't a **nightingale** nor a **lark**. If he wanted to be my Romeo, then he'd have to quickly change the bird! I giggled. I started to enjoy the game of hide and seek. Just you wait, I'll **outsmart** you!

I decided I knew roughly where he was hiding, and when he cried his **mating call** again, I quietly crept up to the bookcase where I thought he was taking cover. He was obviously perplexed that I didn't answer him because his calls came more and more **frequently**. I was now so close. I was quite sure that he was standing opposite me on the other side of the bookcase.

I carefully took a book off the shelf and **peeked** through the narrow gap that it left open. I was right. There he was, **lying in wait**, only an arm's length away, with strangely **pouted lips**, whistling the call of an owl. I could have died with laughter! If I'd had a camera, my photo would definitely have been amongst the winners of our local newspaper's **snapshot contest**.

For some reason the whole thing reminded me of a scene from the film *Romeo and Juliet* – the one when the two main characters see each other for the first time through an aquarium. The only difference was we

---

to play hide and seek – Verstecken spielen;
nightingale – Nachtigall; lark – Lerche;
to outsmart – überlisten; mating call – Balzruf;
frequently – häufig; to peek – spähen; to lie in wait – lauern;
to pout one's lips – die Lippen spitzen;
snapshot contest – Foto-Wettbewerb

weren't separated by a load of colourful fish, but by some big old books! I was just thinking about what to do next when the books in front of me started moving by themselves. I managed to jump back just in time and saved myself from having half the contents of the bookshelf land on my head. At least twenty books crashed to my feet.

"Are you crazy?" I shrieked **in dismay**. "Are you trying to kill me?"

I looked up from the **disarray** at my feet and saw his cheeky face through the new **hole** in the bookshelf. He was grinning at me. He'd obviously thought of the same scene from *Romeo and Juliet* as I did because, with a slightly ironic undertone, he starting **reciting** from the play: "My lips, two blushing **pilgrims**, ready stand / to smooth that rough touch with a tender kiss."

Not bad. How did Juliet respond to that again? "You're not a pilgrim," I said.

"And you're not a **saint**." He took one of the remaining books off the shelf and pressed it to his lips. "Take my kiss with this book ..."

No, how poetic! Didn't Romeo and Juliet kiss for the first time like that? I felt the blood rush to my **cheeks**. An exquisite **shiver** ran though my body. All I had to do was press my lips to the book ... and my happiness would be complete ... the **bond** of love between us tied.

I was just raising the **consecrated tome** to my lips when

---

in dismay – entsetzt; disarray – Unordnung; hole – Loch, Lücke;
to recite – deklamieren; pilgrim – Pilger; saint – Heilige;
cheek – Wange; shiver – Schauder; bond – Band;
consecrated tome – der geweihte Wälzer

I noticed the title of the book: *Studies into the **Inferiority** of the Female Sex: Evidence that Women are not Human. Reprint of a **Doctoral Dissertation** from the Year 1595.*

I broke into loud laughter and threw the book at his head. He managed to **duck** just before the book hit him.

"What's the matter?" he stuttered in bewilderment.

"Read it yourself!" I cried and ran to the door.

"Stop!"

"Catch me if you can!"

And I slammed the door shut behind me as I ran out of the library.

At the same time the school bell rang. It was the end of the break.

Franzi was **impressed** and came to a realistic **conclusion**.

"So you're meeting up with him tomorrow at the drinks dispenser. **Far out**!"

I thought so, too, and I gave a slightly confused sigh. "I can't explain it, Franzi, but the guy just **bowled** me **over**!"

Franzi grinned. "You seem to have your feet firmly on the ground to me!"

I grinned as well. "On the outside, Franzi, only on the outside. Inside I'm lying flat on my face feeling utterly flabbergasted and I don't understand the world anymore!"

---

inferiority – Minderwertigkeit;
doctoral dissertation – Doktorarbeit; to duck – sich ducken;
impressed – beeindruckt; conclusion – Schlussfolgerung;
far out! – echt irre!; to bowl sb over – jmdn. umhauen

Franzi put on a serious **expression** and shook her head slowly. "I'm afraid symptoms like that can only lead to one diagnosis," she said. "You're head-over-heels in love! I recommend **bed rest** and a **cold compress**!"

I grabbed her shoulders and shook her. "You – you beast, you!" I cried, and we ran off to catch the bus laughing.

Before I set about doing the "special tasks" – written punishments – at home, I wanted to wash the smell of school out of my skin. As I approached the shower, I heard loud music. I cautiously opened the door and froze as if struck by lightning. There was a ghetto blaster on the toilet seat blaring out a song by the *Gorillaz* at full volume. I could just make out the Joker under the shower through the steaming **mist**. He was pouring a bottle of malt beer down his throat, **thinking he was the bees' knees**. As I came in, he screamed hysterically and quickly put his hand over his you-know-what.

"Man, don't be so silly!" I snapped, angry at how he'd completely taken over the shower. "Looking won't do you any **harm**! Whatever there is to see!"

He shouted "bitch!" and I slammed the door and withdrew to my desk feeling **thoroughly** frustrated.

I sat **brooding over** the special tasks given to me by Logel and Mrs Ingrimm, but the truth was I spent the

---

expression – Gesichtsausdruck; bed rest – Bettruhe;
cold compress – ein kalter Umschlag; mist – Nebel;
he thinks he's the bees' knees – er hält sich für den Größten;
harm – Schaden; thoroughly – völlig; to brood over – grübeln

whole time thinking about the memorable meeting with the boy from the Year 9. I really regretted not having asked him his name. How annoying! It was a bit strange to be thinking about someone whose name I didn't even know. Maybe I should call Daphne or Fabian. They were both class reps as well, and they probably had a list of the **school council** with all the class reps on it. Bootlicker or macho? What a choice! And what **unsuspecting** reason could I come up with for why I needed the name of the class rep from the Year 9? Think! Think!

I took out the class list from underneath my desktop and dialled Daphne's number. At least she was a girl and **thereby the lesser** of two **evils**. But she didn't answer. Shit! So, Fabian.

"Hi, it's Kristina here …"

"Oh, what an **honour**! To what do I owe this call?"

Sure, it was obvious he'd be **bolshy** with me to begin with.

"Er, well, you don't actually **deserve** an honour like this …" Crikey, what was I saying? That was a bad start for getting information out of him, even if he did take it as a joke.

"… Er, I mean, of course, you deserve it …"

NO! Had I **taken leave of my senses**? That wouldn't work either.

It sounded like he thought the same because, with a

---

school council – Schülerrat; unsuspecting – unverdächtig; thereby – dadurch; the lesser evil – das geringere Übel; honour – Ehre; bolshy – patzig; to deserve – verdienen; to take leave of one's senses – den Verstand verlieren

touch of **impatience** in his voice, he said, "Whether I deserve it or not, what do you want? I have to go to training in a minute."

I took a deep breath. "Could you tell me who the class rep of 9c is?" I managed to **squeeze out**. So, there. I'd said it.

"What do you want to know that for?" came the **inevitable** counter-question.

Yes, quite, why did I want to know? I couldn't exactly tell him the real reason. Perhaps I'd come up with an idea while talking …

"Yes, well …" I started to fall apart. "I – I found a **folder** …" Finding a folder is good, I thought, but what's in it? Why should the class rep get it and not the caretaker who runs the **lost property office**? "You see, the word ***confidential*** is on it …" Confidential was great. That way I didn't have to know what was in the folder. After all, a **respectable** person like me didn't poke her nose into a folder marked with confidential. "Yeah, and *class rep 9c* is on it, too. And because you're also class rep and on the student council, I thought you'd know the name of the class rep from 9c, and then I can give the folder back …"

Phew! Made it! It even sounded pretty **credible**.

"The class rep is called Mariam, Mariam Feldbach. Her dad's a dentist."

---

impatience – Ungeduld; to squeeze out – hervorpressen;
inevitable – unvermeidlich; folder – Mappe;
lost property office – Fundbüro; confidential – vertraulich;
respectable – anständig; credible – glaubwürdig

A girl? Was he **taking the mickey** or what? I knew perfectly well that the class rep from 9c was a boy!

"But the **handwriting** on the folder is definitely from a boy, not from a girl. I can tell," I said, trying to **coax** the name of the boy out of him.

But Fabian just **chuckled** and replied, "Maybe the folder belongs to a girl who writes like a boy. Mariam has a very deep voice …" He took a dramatic pause. "… Or are you just hoping the folder **belongs** to a boy?"

"No, no, not at all," I said quickly, but at the same time I couldn't help thinking: what a disaster! To try and **smooth** things **over** I quickly added, "I expect you're right. A girl with a deep voice probably has a handwriting like a boy, too."

"Yeah, well, if all you ever think about is boys …" **said** Fabian **disparagingly**. "I have to go to football now. Ciao!"

And – whoosh – the line was dead.

Mariam Feldbach. OK then, I'd try my luck with her. And she did, in fact, give me the required information **without beating about the bush**.

"Thanks," I said. "That's really nice of you."

I sat back down at my desk and before I knew it, there was a huge blue ink heart on the cover of my Maths exercise book. And in the middle of the heart was the name "Meik".

---

to take the mickey – jmdn. aufziehen; handwriting – Handschrift; to coax – entlocken; to chuckle – kichern; to belong – gehören; to smooth over – geradebiegen; to say sth disparagingly – lästern; without beating about the bush – ohne Umschweife

# Competition is good for business

The next day at main break I was strolling over to the gym **single-mindedly**, when all of a sudden my feet stopped in their tracks and my breath stuck in my throat. I couldn't believe what I was seeing! But, unfortunately, the sight before me was not some bright, shimmering **mirage**, but the grey, **remorseless** reality. The class rep of 9c was standing in front of the drinks dispenser **as arranged**, but – as was not arranged – Mona was standing next to him.

And she wasn't standing next to him because she was just getting something to drink from the dispenser. No. She already had a bottle in her hand and was obviously having a nice little chat with him, only interrupting the flow of conversation when she sucked on the straw of her drink. I could hear her girly giggles **wafting** over to me through the air.

"I'll kill her," I hissed to Franzi, "if she comes on to Meik, I'll strangle her and make her **choke** on that stupid laugh of hers."

---

single-mindedly – zielstrebig; mirage – Fata Morgana; remorseless – unerbittlich; as arranged – wie verabredet; to waft – wehen; to choke – ersticken

Franzi looked at me **disapprovingly** in the face of this sudden **outburst** of aggression.

"Don't **take the law into your own hands**!" she warned. "And no uncontrolled acts of **violence**! Let me deal with this." She pushed me to one side and headed straight over towards the two of them.

Oh no! What was she going to do? She wasn't going to make a fool of me in front of Meik, was she?

But she handled the situation really coolly. "Oh, Mona," she said. "There you are. Mr Wolf is looking for you. He needs to speak to you **urgently**. Something to do with your papers, I think."

I chuckled to myself. I expect the **clearance certificate** was missing. She probably had a number of **previous convictions** for **unscrupulous** flirting in schoolyards!

"Then we'll just have to end our nice conversation – unfortunately," Mona said, glancing regretfully at Meik. "But maybe we can continue it on the bus."

All of a sudden, her face lit up like a Christmas tree. Her smile had more **voltage** than Time Square. She sighed "Ciao!" to Meik and headed off towards the **administration block**.

And what did Meik do? He just stared at her like she was some model on a **catwalk**.

---

disapprovingly – missbilligend; outburst – Ausbruch;
to take the law into one's own hand – Selbstjustiz üben;
violence – Gewalt; urgently – dringend;
clearance certificate – polizeiliches Führungszeugnis;
previous conviction – Vorstrafe; unscrupulous – skrupellos;
voltage – [elektrische] Spannung;
administration block – Verwaltungstrakt; catwalk – Laufsteg

I couldn't really blame him. The way she swung those **hips** of hers on the end of her long legs, well, she really was like some catwalk babe, I guess. I sighed. A sight like that must really **give** the boys **a kick**.

All of a sudden, a wave of resignation came over me. If I now went up to Meik to talk to him, he'd probably end up comparing me to her. And I knew how I would **fare** if he did. I stood upright, stuck out my **chest** and walked towards Meik with swaying hips, trying to look at least a little bit like a model.

He spotted me straightaway. "Oh, hello, I'm glad you remembered our meeting. I …" He stopped all of a sudden and stared at me. "Have you hurt yourself?"

"Me? Hurt myself? No, why?"

He still looked a bit **worried**. "I thought something was wrong with your hips. You were walking so strangely."

Franzi had to quickly hold her hand up to her mouth to **smother** an uncontrolled burst of laughter. She'd obviously **grasped** straightaway that I was trying to impress him with my stylish way of walking. He didn't, of course. He hadn't grasped anything. And he wasn't impressed either. But at least he showed some concern about me, that was something. I relaxed into my normal **posture** and went back to walking normally.

"No, I'm alright. I just **strained** myself **lifting** something, that's all."

---

hip – Hüfte; to give sb a kick – jmdn. antörnen;
to fare – [er]gehen, abschneiden; chest – Brustkorb;
worried – besorgt; to smother – ersticken; to grasp – kapieren;
posture – [Körper]haltung; to strain – zerren; to lift – heben

"Hopefully not the books I was carrying yesterday," he said with a grin and offered me a short surf on the wave of sympathy.

I jumped up. "Who knows ..."

"Well, then I'm even more **indebted to** you. Can I repay you with a Coke, or is that too little?"

"It's a start," I said, feeling more **courageous**.

He paid for a bottle from the dispenser, removed the cap and held it out to me with a straw.

"Do you want one as well ..." he turned to Franzi, who had been watching the scene with wide open eyes.

But before she could answer, I spoke for her. "Didn't you want to help Lea with her Biology homework? She's been waiting for you for ten minutes. Break's over in a minute."

Franzi didn't exactly look at me in a friendly manner, but she turned down the Coke with thanks and disappeared.

Alone with Meik at last!

He also took a Coke, and then we stood in front of the drinks dispenser together and didn't say a word.

I couldn't help thinking that he was probably thinking about Mona. "What are you thinking about?" I asked. The question came out of my mouth without any warning. Couldn't I control myself? It was so embarrassing to start a conversation like that again.

"I was just **wondering** if you were in the same class as Mona," he said.

---

to be indebted to sb – in jmds. Schuld stehen; courageous – mutig; to wonder – sich etwas fragen

My ears started to buzz like I was standing under the Niagara Falls. **At any rate**, it was like taking a really cold shower. How did he know her name? And what did he care which class she was in? She'd obviously managed to wrap him around her little finger already. What did she say again? *Maybe we can continue this conversation on the bus.* That was just my luck: I'd finally met a really nice guy, and he just had to take the same bus as that silly cow! Come on, fate, I moaned, that's really not fair! I sucked at my straw with all the sucking power I had in me. He didn't fail to notice this.

"You've got a lot of **puff**!" he commented with a grin.

I would normally have found his comment really sweet, but in this competitive situation I felt like I had **dropped my guard** again. I had to make up for that quickly. "Hum, no, er, I mean, yes … it's hot today!"

A look of amazement **darted** across his face again. That was hardly surprising: it wasn't hot at all that day. On the contrary, it was far too cold for that time of year. How embarrassing!

I expect he thought I had a **hot flush** now. He'd probably had enough of me already. First I **limped** my way up to him, then I got a hot flush, and now I couldn't even come up with a sentence that made sense. He must have taken me for a **dumb blonde**. I couldn't understand why everything was so different from the day before. It had

---

at any rate – jedenfalls; puff – Zug;
to drop one's guard – sich eine Blöße geben; to dart – huschen;
hot flush – Hitzewallung; to limp – hinken;
dumb blonde – blöde Blondine

been so nice and **trouble-free**. It was all that Mona's fault. I worked myself up into a **rage** about the new girl. If she hadn't have tried to creep up to him, then everything would be much better now. While I was thinking about how I could **conjure up** the funky vibes from yesterday, three of the older boys suddenly came up to us.

"Alright, **mate**? Trying your luck with someone from Year 7, are we?" one of them said ironically and poked Meik in the ribs.

The other one looked at me from head to toe and whistled through his teeth. "Not a bad **bit of skirt**," he said, "if you're into **toddler**!"

To which the third boy burst into **raucous** laughter and snorted, "I didn't know you worked as a babysitter, Meik! You kill me, you do!"

Meik now seemed to find the situation extremely embarrassing. I was really interested to see how he'd react. I thought he would **deny** me like Peter. And I was right. Before the **cock crowed** three times – or in this case, before the school bell rang – he said to me, "OK, take care. If the drinks dispenser breaks again, just call Uncle Meik!" And with a stupid laugh and an **artificial** "cheers" he raised his bottle to his lips and drank it in one go. Then he **tossed** the empty bottle into the bin and headed off with his mates from Year 9.

---

trouble-free – problemlos; rage – Zorn;
to conjure up – herbeizaubern; mate – Kumpel, Alter;
a bit of skirt – (ugs.) Mädchen; toddler – Kleinkind;
raucous – heiser; to deny – verleugnen; cock – Hahn;
to crow – krähen; artificial – gekünstelt; to toss – werfen

I was **on the brink of tears**. He hadn't even asked me my name.

"She *is* a witch!" I said to Franzi on the way home. "She only needs to look at boys and they come under her spell. She would have been burned alive in the **Middle Ages**!"

And **rightly so**, as far as I was concerned.

But Franzi just said dryly, "Cool down, girl. If you didn't always behave like a rabbit in front of a snake when she's around, then you'd have more luck with boys. You're ruining your chances with your jealousy. Concentrate on your positive qualities instead of comparing yourself to her all the time. Competition can be good for business if you handle it in the right way!"

Franzi again. She might be able to study **Business Management** later in life with an opinion like that, but she couldn't **improve** my mood. She really wasn't an expert in psychology.

And so I **trudged** home from the bus stop feeling completely depressed.

"Oh, leave me alone," I said to Sniffy as she jumped up to me when I came through the door. "I'm not in the mood to play."

That didn't stop her from licking my hand before she **scampered off** into the corner of the room, her tail between her legs. At least she noticed straightaway that I'd

---

on the brink of tears – den Tränen nah; Middle Ages – Mittelalter; rightly so – zu Recht; Business Management – Betriebswirtschaft; to improve – verbessern; to trudge – schleichen, trotten; to scamper off – wegflitzen

**got out of bed on the wrong side**. I couldn't say the same for the rest of my family. I was just happy that my brother was out with a friend that day and was going to sleep over at his place. One pain in the neck less.

I was just about to start my Art homework when the scene with Meik at the drinks dispenser came into my mind again. He'd simply denied knowing me when his mates turned up. As if I was too stupid to get a Coke out of the dispenser. I **scribbled** the piece of paper in front of me full. If Mona had been standing next to him at the time, then Meik would probably have introduced her to his mates and **bragged** about his **conquest**. He was probably just playing a game with me.

I called Franzi. "I can't just let Mona have him," I said, feeling frustrated. "But how am I meant **to win him over** when he's not the least bit interested in me?"

Franzi saw things realistically as usual. "Well, first of all, you have to **get rid of** your Mona-phobia. She's here now, and there's nothing you can do about it. But that doesn't mean that you have to keep comparing yourself to her."

"I don't. But why does she always have to turn up where I am and always do what I'm doing? It's enough to **drive** me **crazy**!"

---

to get out of bed on the wrong side – mit dem linken Fuß zuerst aufstehen; to scribble – kritzeln; to brag – prahlen;
conquest – Eroberung; to win sb over – jmdn. für sich gewinnen;
to get rid of sth – etwas loswerden;
to drive sb crazy – jmdn. zum Wahnsinn treiben

Franzi obviously began to grasp that my **despair** was absolutely genuine because she then said sympathetically, "That's true. Even for my taste you two seem to **cross paths** a bit too often. Perhaps you're just too **similar**."

I wasn't hearing properly.

"Too similar? What possible similarities do I have with her?" I wasn't brunette, I was blonde. And my nose was much smaller than hers.

"I don't mean the way you look. I'm talking about your interests. The same study-groups, the same taste in boys, that kind of thing. That means you **bump into** each other. I expect she doesn't mean it."

Whether she meant it or not, it was starting to get on my nerves.

I made myself a tea and had to admit that Franzi was right. Mona was surprisingly similar to me. Not only had she chosen the same study-groups, she was also good in the same subjects as me and she seemed to like the same teachers as me as well. At least she **sucked up to** my favourite teachers without any scruples. Oh yes, and when it came to boys, we obviously had the same taste, too. Well, at least that's the impression I got in the case of Meik – after all, anyone who started something with one of the *Gorilla* boys was obviously suffering from a severe

---

despair – Verzweiflung;
to cross sb's path – jmdn. über den Weg laufen; similar – ähnlich;
to bump into – zufällig begegnen;
to suck up to sb – sich bei jmdm. einschleimen

**lack of taste**. *There's a monkey in the jungle and its brain is in its tail ...*

Fabian, Sebastian, Snorkel ... she could have them all. I was generous when it came to them. But she should leave her grubby hands off Meik.

It soon **occurred to** me that Mona's **rivalry** wasn't my only problem. I didn't actually have a plan to win over Meik. After all, he was in Year 9, and he probably thought I was just as green as his mates did. I expected he hadn't wasted another thought on me after his little **slip-up** in the library.

How tragic. Was there really no way I could reach him?

Something **rattled** at the front door. Sniffy barked and Mum made her usual entrance by coming through the door like a **whirlwind**. Why did I have to have such a hyperactive mother? She was always buzzing for action, sometimes I found it really **distressing**. The front door had only just closed behind her and Sniffy had stopped barking her welcome, when she burst into my room and started **talking nineteen to the dozen** to me.

"Can you spare me a cup of tea? Yes? Then I'll get myself a cup." And she was off again, but continued to talk at full volume from the kitchen: "I've brought some **raspberry gateau** with me. Do you want a piece?"

---

lack of taste – Geschmacksverirrung;
to occur to sb – jmdm. klar werden; rivalry – Rivalität;
slip-up – Ausrutscher; to rattle – klappern;
whirlwind – Wirbelwind; distressing – quälend;
to talk nineteen to the dozen – reden wie ein Wasserfall;
raspberry gateau – Himbeertörtchen

Without waiting for me to answer, she came swirling back into my room a few seconds later balancing her cup and two plates of cake. She put everything down on the large, round tea tray and dropped herself down next to me on the sofa bed.

"My goodness!" she groaned. "That was some day! But it was really interesting. I managed to get a phenomenal project for the agency today: the whole **advertising campaign** for the **fashion show** in the City-Centre. Advertising **pillars** and **billboards**, advertising in the press, cinema and sports arenas, and the design and construction of the catwalk." She rubbed her hands together in delight.

"Congratulations," I said and took my plate of raspberry gateau without any real emotion. Mum was this enthusiastic about nearly all her jobs at the beginning. But as the fork full of cake was about to enter my mouth, I suddenly realised the real meaning of what she'd just said. Did Mum just mention a *fashion show*? That sounded really interesting. At least, better than advertising for **DIY superstores** and old people's homes. Perhaps I could learn a few tricks about styling from them.

I lowered the fork from my lips and let the cake be a cake.

"Did you just say fashion show?" I asked curiously.

She looked **thrilled** by the fact that I was showing

---

advertising campaign – Werbekampagne;
fashion show – Modenschau; pillar – Säule;
billboard – Reklametafel;
DIY (Do-it-yourself) superstore – Baumarkt; thrilled – erfreut

some interest in her work. I should **add** that this wasn't always the case.

"Yes. You know. The big spring and summer fashion show in the City-Centre. All the boutiques in the Centre take part, from teeny-fashion to fashion for **plump** ladies."

I giggled. "Maybe you should **apply** to be a model."

My mum – who wasn't exactly as **thin as a rake** – sighed with playful theatricality and stuffed the rest of the cake into her mouth **undaunted**.

"That's not for me," she said. "I've got too much on my hands with all the advertising. We want to arrange the show differently this time. With a model competition and models from the street. Laymen – or girls – I should say. We need teens your age."

I couldn't believe my ears! Was Mum going completely mad? What was I supposed to do at a fashion show? Make a fool of myself?

"Why should you make a fool of yourself?" Mum couldn't understand my **reservations**. "You're good-looking, and it can't be that difficult to walk along a catwalk with a few pretty things on."

"You're forgetting that everybody looks at you while you're doing it! That's mega-embarrassing."

My mum **swallowed** the remains of the raspberry gateau and washed it down with some blackberry tea. "I

---

to add – dazusagen; plump – vollschlank;
to apply – sich bewerben; thin as a rake – gertenschlank;
undaunted – unverzagt; reservation – Vorbehalt;
to swallow – schlucken

hadn't looked at it like that. I thought it would be fun for a young girl like you. Oh well, I guess when you're caught up in puberty, you're just more **touchy** about these things. It was just an idea. We'll get enough **applicants**. After all, the winner and **runners-up** get a shopping **voucher**."

That couldn't **tempt** me either. It was highly **unlikely** that I would be one of the winners, so there wasn't even any point participating. Watching a bit and getting a few tips wasn't such a bad idea though.

As I lay in bed that evening, I couldn't help thinking again of the frustrating scene from that morning. And try as I might to **dispel** those images from my mind, I just couldn't do it. I kept seeing Mona **strutting** along a catwalk like a model, her head held high and her hips swinging. It must be possible to learn to walk like that, I thought, and I asked myself if Mum's fashion show might be the ideal opportunity. I clambered out of my bed and **fumbled** my way to my parents' bedroom in my pyjamas. Mum slept alone there at the moment because Dad was at a conference in Berlin.

The light was still on. Mum was sitting in bed, her **writing board** propped up on her knees, drafting plans for advertising ideas.

---

touchy – empfindlich; applicant – Bewerber;
the runners-up – die weiteren Plätze; voucher – Gutschein;
to tempt – verlocken; unlikely – unwahrscheinlich;
to dispel – verscheuchen; to strut – stolzieren; to fumble – tapern;
writing board – Schreibbrett

"Come in," she said when she heard me cautiously opening the door. "You're not disturbing me. What do you think of this slogan? 'Your city flyer – Taxi Meier'? Or: 'Taxi Meier takes you higher'? I can picture a taxi flying over the city where all the roads are **clogged up** with cars …" She saw the sceptical look in my eyes. "Bad idea? OK, I'll work at it. It's for the cinema advertising. Can I help you by the way?"

"Er, yes, but it's not that important really …"

"It can't be all that *un*important either. Otherwise you wouldn't come into my room so late."

"That's true," I **admitted**. "I was just thinking about a few things. This fashion show where you're doing the advertising, how's it going to work exactly? You can't just pick a few girls out of schools, put them in some **fancy** clothes and throw them onto the catwalk."

Mum giggled at this dramatic image. "No, of course not. First of all there's a casting where the most talented girls and boys will be picked out. Then a professional agency will train them to do a kind of choreography for the fashion show – with music **and all that jazz**."

Now I really was **intrigued**.

"What do you mean by 'all that jazz'?" I asked inquisitively. "Like how to move your body like a model? How to walk with style? So that everyone looks at you?"

Mum laughed. "Of course! That's the whole **point**. Every model wants the people around her to look at her

---

clogged up – verstopft; to admit – zugeben; fancy – nobel; and all that jazz – und all so was; intrigued – sehr neugierig; point – (hier:) Sinn

and the things she's presenting. I'm sure **practising** how to walk up and down the catwalk elegantly will be one of the exercises."

"Groovy!" The word just slipped out. Mum looked at me in surprise. "Do you think it's difficult to learn something like that?"

Mum shrugged her shoulders. "No idea. I expect you need a bit of talent as well. I guess you have to be comfortable with your own body ... have a bit of self-confidence ... maybe even a feel for music ... That probably all helps."

Hm. My musicality certainly had its limits, but I was good at sport and gymnastics. I was rather lacking in self-confidence, especially since Mona had turned up. But hey! Maybe being able to walk perfectly would help **boost** it a bit.

"Do you think I could learn it?"

Mum **saw through** me straightaway. "Aha, are you interested?"

"If I do apply, then it will only be because of the **character-building** aspect."

Mum was **gobsmacked**. "Because of *what*?"

"You know, I wouldn't do it for all that modelling **lark**, but for the way it could help me with my self-confidence. You know, because I **dared** to do it!"

---

to practise – üben; to boost – steigern;
to see through sb – jmdn. durchschauen;
character-building – persönlichkeitsbildend;
gobsmacked – verblüfft; lark – Tamtam;
to dare – wagen, sich trauen

"Aha," said Mum. "I hadn't looked at it like that. I just thought it would be a bit of fun for young girls like you, dressing up in clothes that your parents normally can't **afford** and performing to the latest music."

I laughed. Yes, that was typical Mum! A real action girl! Having fun? Well, I suppose she was right. If I learned to walk with as much **finesse** as Mona, I'd be the centre of attention in the schoolyard. If all the boys ended up looking at me after the fashion show, then it would be fun for me as well. Meik would probably be really impressed. He'd **fall over himself to** get a date with me. Yes, that's the way things would probably work out.

In the bathroom the following morning I **inspected** myself closely in the mirror. Was I pretty enough to apply to be a model? I wasn't ugly but I wasn't particularly **striking** either but that didn't necessarily have to be a negative thing. I certainly had very nice blonde hair. I was glad I didn't have as many **spots** as Franzi. You could see she was going through puberty miles away. Sometimes she looked like a **crumble cake**. It always amazed me how **casually** she took it. I wouldn't even have dared to show my face in public. On the **contrary**. I would probably have run off to a **convent**.

---

to afford – sich leisten; finesse – Geschick;
to fall over oneself to do sth – sich um etwas reißen;
to inspect – begutachten; striking – auffällig; spot – Pickel;
crumble cake – Streuselkuchen; casually – lässig;
contrary – Gegenteil; convent – Kloster

I finished in the bathroom and went to the breakfast table, where I made myself a slice of toast.

When Mum joined me with a morning greeting, I looked at her **resolutely** and said with a determined voice, "You can bring me a **registration form** when the time comes. Perhaps they really might take me."

In school Franzi had to immediately tell the other *Pepper Dollies* about my problem with Meik. Had I **given** her **the go-ahead**?

"Oh, don't make such a fuss," she played down my **complaint**. "Your worries are our worries!"

And Greetje giggled, "We're here to help you!"

"What makes you so sure that the guy is worth it?" asked Lea. "He's not that good-looking."

I shrugged my shoulders, meaning: I don't know. That **infamous** little guy with a **bow and arrow** – the one whose job it is to cause chaos amongst the human race – must have been wandering through our schoolyard just at the moment when Meik put his stack of books down next to me on the bench. I still turned hot and cold when I thought of the way he'd looked at me with those blue eyes of his. And when I thought about the scene in the library, I almost **lost the thread** completely.

---

resolutely – entschlossen;
registration form – Anmeldeformular;
to give the go-ahead – grünes Licht geben;
complaint – Beschwerde; infamous – berüchtigt;
bow and arrow – Pfeil und Bogen;
to lose the thread – den Faden verlieren

"It is the way it is," I said. "**Cupid hit the bull's eye** with me!"

"Oh my goodness!" groaned Greetje. "**You've got it really bad**!"

"And what are we going to do now?" Franzi asked looking for a realistic and concrete solution to my problem. "How can Kiki win him over?"

Silence.

"Couldn't you ask him for a date for me?" I suggested to Franzi.

"Am I your **harbinger** of love or something? No way!" the **rejection** came promptly.

"All we need to do is find out if there's a party going on somewhere," said Lea. "Then you could take him along."

"*If* he lets me take him along. I doubt he's into Year 7 parties."

"I expect he's already forgotten me anyway," I moaned. "He doesn't even know my name."

"Not the best conditions," said Lea, making me feel even more depressed.

"I should just give up on him," I sighed. "Mona can have him. I don't stand a chance anyway."

"We could **mug** him, tie him up and **gag** him, and take him away to some romantic place," suggested Franzi **light-heartedly**, trying to help me get out of my bad

---

cupid – Amor; to hit the bull's eye – ins Schwarze treffen; You've got it really bad! – Dich hat es schlimm erwischt!; harbinger – Bote; rejection – Ablehnung; to mug – überfallen; to gag – knebeln; light-heartedly – heiter

mood. "Or you could **appeal** to his sympathy. Class reps have a natural **social bent**. Throw yourself at his feet, **faint** or break down in tears and stutter something **incomprehensible**. Then he'll take you to the medical room and you'll have him all to yourself."

That was going a bit too far for me.

"For crying out loud, people, life isn't a soap opera! And I'm anything but a good actor. I'd burst into laughter not tears!"

"Alright, girl," said Franzi, "then there's nothing we can do!"

I arrived home with an absolutely delightful feeling of being completely **incapable** and helpless when it came to **relationships**. As I took the post out of the letter box, I saw that there was a letter for me. I was slightly confused by the sender's address on the back of the **envelope**: The Berger Agency, Berlin? Probably some stupid advert.

I unlocked the door, said hello to Sniffy and put the post to one side. At some point later I walked past the telephone and spotted the letter again. I opened it **absent-mindedly**. I **inattentively** ran my eyes over the first few lines. No! I couldn't believe it! It was from the modelling agency who were organising the fashion show in the

---

to appeal – appellieren; a social bent – eine soziale Ader;
to faint – ohnmächtig werden;
incomprehensible – unverständlich; incapable – unfähig;
relationship – Beziehung; envelope – Briefumschlag;
absent-mindedly – geistesabwesend;
inattentively – unkonzentriert

City-Centre! They were actually inviting me to a casting. I thought I was going to die! It was absolutely amazing!! I shouted for joy and – **in the absence of** a human being to hug – I grabbed Sniffy and **squeezed** her tight until she **squealed**. I put her down and danced around half the house while she barked like crazy around me.

It was all completely mad. I, Kristina Siebert, was invited to a model casting. Mum would make eyes for sure!

She was – as I guessed – **over the moon** for me, but all she said was, "I didn't doubt it for a second." Very cool.

I was amazed by her **self-assurance** which only made me wonder if she'd **had a hand in it**. In any case, my own self-confidence suddenly got a major **boost** and, as I dropped into bed that evening, I thought optimistically: "Just you wait, Meiki! I'll get you!"

When I told the *Pepper Dollies* about the casting the next day, they all thought I was completely off my rocker.

"Do you want to become a brain-dead fashion **chick** now, or what?" asked Franzi critically.

And Lea said, "Just don't become a **megalomaniac**."

I could partly understand them because, like my friends, I'd never had anything to do with fashion and make-up and all that **razzamatazz**. Until now I'd always

---

in the absence of – in Ermangelung von; to squeeze – drücken; to squeal – quieken; to be over the moon – überglücklich sein; self-assurance – Selbstsicherheit;
to have a hand in it – die Hand im Spiel haben; boost – Auftrieb; chick – Tussi; megalomaniac – Größenwahnsinnige/r; razzamatazz – Schnickschnack

thought it was all just a **facade**. People define themselves through their inner qualities. It was just bad luck if nobody noticed them! But perhaps you had to **polish** the facade a bit as well.

*Get the cool, get the cool shoeshine* ... the grinning Chinese boy from the *Gorillaz'* hit sang into my ear. His mum was of the strange opinion that you had more chances in life with polished shoes. OK, shoes alone these days weren't **the be-all and end-all**, but in principle it was true: after all, that **dolled-up** Mona hit it off with the boys in no time at all. I had to do something about the situation, and I saw it as an **act of providence** that my mother had brought this fashion show to my attention.

"Listen, people," I said, "it was my mum's tip, and I reckon it'll be really cool. After all, the whole **gig** is going to be **rehearsed** by real professionals. You should apply as well. Then we can have fun all together!"

Blimey, my friends were experts at laughing in a silly way, but they didn't have enough **guts** to apply.

"OK," they finally gave me their **blessing**. "The main thing is you don't mutate into a catwalk chick!"

I was able to reassure them there. "Of course, I won't. Just look at it as a ... a social experiment."

They looked at me with wide open eyes. And their **jaws** dropped to the floor. Was I being too academic for them?

---

facade – Fassade; to polish – polieren;
the be-all and end-all – das Ein und Alles; dolled-up – aufgemotzt;
act of providence – eine Fügung des Schicksals;
gig – Veranstaltung; to rehearse – proben; guts – Mumm;
blessing – Segen; jaw – Kiefer

"Look, I just reckon I can learn a lot about people on the catwalk and behind the scenes."

"I bet," said Franzi and she added almost **clairvoyantly**, "and I'm sure a lot about yourself, too."

The casting day finally arrived. "Do you really think I can go to it?" I don't know how many times I'd asked Mum this question, but if I was getting on her nerves, she didn't show it at all.

"Of course, you can. You're a nice-looking girl," she said **patiently**. "You're every mother's dream of a 13-year-old daughter … like the **proverbial** girl next door."

Yeah, thanks a lot. If that was meant to be a compliment, then it didn't really make me feel any better. I mean, who wants to be the ordinary girl next door? If I was going to participate in a fashion show, then I'd rather be a shooting star – maybe even the **undiscovered** beauty from the provinces – but not the boring girl next door! No way! Mum got some funny things into her head sometimes. But at least my brother boosted my confidence a bit.

As I came out of the bathroom, he gave me a **grunt** of **acknowledgement**, put his bottle of malt beer to his lips and, after taking a big gulp, said, "Way out, sis, you look funky-dory!" I didn't exactly know what he was talking about because I wasn't too familiar with Year 5 slang, but I could tell it was a compliment by the tone of his voice.

---

clairvoyantly – hellsichtig; patiently – geduldig;
proverbial – sprichwörtlich; undiscovered – unentdeckt;
grunt – Grunzen; acknowledgement – Anerkennung

He must have spotted the lack of **comprehension** in my eyes because, in a slightly **patronizing** tone, he quickly added, "They're bound to pick you. You'll make the rest of them look old."

I just had to give him a big **hug** after that. He only put up a bit of **resistance**.

"Come on, lean over," he then said. "Let me **spit** over your shoulder. Then nothing can go wrong."

I **obediently** leaned forward and, standing **on his tiptoes**, he spat over my shoulder three times. "Good luck and **break a leg**!"

---

comprehension – Verständnis; patronizing – gönnerhaft;
hug – Umarmung; resistance – Widerstand; to spit – spucken;
obediently – gehorsam; on tiptoes – auf Zehenspitzen;
break a leg! – Hals- und Beinbruch!

## Who's the most beautiful of them all?

But spitting didn't do the job that day. Or else I just belonged to the people who **attract** chaos like a **lightning conductor** attracts lightning.

A casting session isn't such a big deal really. From all the applications they pick out the people who are fairly good-looking and who, on the basis of a certain IQ, they assume are capable of learning. Because about two to three times as many people as needed meet these **prerequisites**, they are invited to a casting. The **selection committee** then gets to meet the people "live" and see how they carry themselves in public. The best are then selected by a jury and are allowed to participate both in the fashion show and the competition for the prizes.

At least that's how I understood it. But there are often worlds between theory and practice.

I was sitting in the bus, **smartly** dressed and **unassumingly** made-up, reading the invitation again nervously. The date and the time were correct. Thursday 19.00 in the open foyer of the City-Centre.

---

to attract – anziehen; lightning conductor – Blitzableiter; prerequisite – Vorbedingung; selection committee – Auswahlkomitee; smartly – schick; unassumingly – dezent

Franzi had her piano lesson, but she wanted to come around straight afterwards. I hoped she would. She had to hold my hand. Otherwise I'd **freak out** with nervousness and do something crazy and auto-aggressive like chew on my fingernails or bite open my lower lip.

Neither activity would exactly improve my **appearance** – more likely reduce my chances. So it was really, really important that Franzi came.

She soon turned up, but it didn't help me at all in the end.

When I arrived at the City-Centre, the place was full of great looking people – of both sexes – who were standing around looking lost. I was surprised. They couldn't all be here for the casting, could they? And they weren't in the end either. Like me, the **would-be** models had all brought along their friends, **relatives** and even parents for moral support. The **latter** were mostly armed with a video or photo camera.

It was a while before I found Franzi in the **crush**. I had only just slipped my hand into hers with a great sense of **relief** and begged her not to leave my side until the end of the casting, when someone started to make an **announcement** over the **tannoy**.

The Centre Manager was on the microphone personally. He was an agile man in his mid-forties, rather

---

to freak out – ausflippen; appearance – Aussehen;
would-be – Möchtegern-; relatives – Verwandte;
the latter – die Letzteren; crush – Gewusel;
relief – Erleichterung; announcement – Durchsage;
tannoy – Lautsprecher

plump, with not a lot of hair on his head, but dressed in an unassuming and businesslike way in a **suit** and tie. "Ladies and gentlemen, dear applicants, boys and girls, I'm delighted to see so many of you here today with your family and friends."

Applause.

"Together with the advertising agency, Siebert & Partner, we've come up with something very special for this year's Spring & Summer Fashion Show. Instead of using professional models, we are inviting YOU – the young people of this town – to present our fashion items and to participate in a modelling competition."

Applause again.

"The fact that we've had over eight hundred applicants from the town and region is proof enough that this idea fell on **fertile** ground."

A **murmur** went through the crowd. Franzi and I looked at each other as well. Over eight hundred applicants! Well, blow me down! And they chose me! I couldn't help admiring myself.

Franzi, it seemed, agreed. "You can already be really proud of yourself!" she said in acknowledgement.

I was. I really was. But I just giggled and waved my hand at her dismissively. Who wants to come across as being conceited?

"Inevitably it's not possible that all applicants take part in the fashion show and, with a heavy heart, we've invited a jury to make a final selection. Not an easy task with so many good-looking young men and women. We

---

suit – Anzug; fertile – fruchtbar; murmur – Raunen

would like to say a big thank you to everyone, even if you are not selected. Thank you for your application. And a round of applause for the courage which you've all shown with your application."

He started to clap and got us to join in, and soon the crowd was clapping as well. It was like a club dance on Mallorca: *"If you're happy on vacation, clap your hands ..."*

He finally **got to the point**. "We've invited sixty male and female applicants here this evening. From these the jury will make the final **selection** of our models."

He went over to a table where I guessed the Jury members were sitting, although I could **hardly** see them through the crowd of people. Each jury member then took the microphone and introduced themselves. They all came from the major clothes shops in the City-Centre, plus the perfume shop on the first floor, the local newspaper and a well-known Berlin modelling agency. The only jury member I could see was the woman from the modelling agency, and I was seriously impressed. She had bright red hair, was at least fifty, rather **corpulent** and exquisitely dressed, not like a businesswoman, more like a gallery owner or theatre-goer. On top of that she was **draped** in jewellery. In an outfit like that a lot of women would have looked like a cleaning lady on their way to the **lonely hearts ball**, but this woman just looked really stylish.

---

to get to the point – zur Sache kommen; selection – Auswahl; hardly – kaum; corpulent – beleibt; to drape – behängen; lonely hearts ball – Ball der einsamen Herzen

"Sixty people," I said to Franzi. "How many do you think they'll **pick**? Do you think I've got a chance at all?"

Franzi looked around. "I don't see why not. There don't seem to be that many girls our age here. Most of them are eighteen or older."

"The advertisement didn't say how old the applicants had to be. They probably all thought it was just a fashion show for adults. If my mum hadn't have told me, I wouldn't have thought of applying either."

"Sshh. Be quiet!" Franzi **prodded** me. "What did he say?"

"... yes, I'm afraid you heard right. I'm sorry to say you're going to have to ask your friends and relatives to please leave the building. We want our future models to feel as relaxed as possible when they present themselves to the jury. Too many **unfamiliar** people watching can be rather **inhibiting**. Please **keep your fingers crossed** at home. If I could ask you all to take your leave now, please."

Then came some discreet music.

I **clung** to Franzi's hand. "You can't go. No way. I won't be able to make it on my own."

"Of course, you'll manage on your own," Franzi tried to **encourage** me, but I was seized by panic and was **convinced** that as soon as I let go of Franzi's hand, I would

---

to pick – auswählen; to prod – anstupsen;
unfamiliar – fremd; inhibiting – hemmend;
to keep one's fingers crossed – die Daumen drücken;
to cling – klammern; to encourage sb – jmdm. Mut machen;
convinced – überzeugt

mutate into a stiff ugly **duckling** who would **wobble** along the catwalk, not stride down it elegantly.

"I'm lost if you go!" I **whimpered**.

But I was going too far, even for Franzi. If there was one thing she hated, it was my occasional habit of feeling excessively **inferior**. "Just stop talking yourself into complexes, will you?" she snapped at me **indignantly**. "The others will get through it on their own, too. Why should you need a babysitter – you of all people?"

That hurt. But it helped me to **get a grip on myself**. It wasn't so difficult to say goodbye to Franzi after that because I spotted a familiar face on one of the upper galleries of the foyer: my mum with a few people from the advertising agency. She seemed to be watching events from there. Even if she couldn't hold my hand, her **presence** alone was moral support enough to make my **separation** from Franzi possible.

She gave me a hug and squeezed a small teddy bear into my hand. "The *Pepper Dollies* asked me to give you this. They wish you all the best and are keeping their fingers crossed for you."

I was **touched**.

Then all the friends and family disappeared, and the Centre Manager invited us to take a seat.

---

duckling – Entlein; to wobble – watscheln;
to whimper – wimmern; inferior – minderwertig;
indignantly – ungehalten;
to get a grip on oneself – sich am Riemen reißen;
presence – Anwesenheit; separation – Trennung;
touched – gerührt

There were several rows of chairs on either side of a **provisional** catwalk which ran **diagonally** through the hall. We all squeezed onto the chairs, but we soon realised there weren't enough for all of us. I wasn't in the mood to argue with someone about where to sit, so I just stood behind the row of chairs with a few other girls and a few guys who looked rather lost.

If modelling was a question of courage, then we girls were obviously the more **gutsy** sex! I could count the number of male applicants on one hand, and they weren't that good-looking either. Meik should have applied, I thought to myself and giggled inside. He had such a lot of charisma.

"We'll call you up alphabetically and ask you to briefly introduce yourselves and take a few steps down the catwalk for us. When everyone's finished, the jury will make its **decision**. About fifteen of you will be picked to take part at our City-Centre Fashion Show. I wish you all the best of luck!"

I was just clapping out of politeness to these words as I found myself looking at the back of a dark head of hair. It belonged to a girl standing with her back to me on the other side of the catwalk. For some reason I had the **sneaking suspicion** that I knew her. All of a sudden, she turned around and I **recognised** her straightaway.

Crikey! I couldn't believe it. It was my old friend, Debbie from **primary school**. She looked fantastic!

---

provisional – provisorisch; diagonally – schräg; gutsy – tapfer; decision – Entscheidung; sneaking suspicion – leiser Verdacht; to recognise – erkennen; primary school – Grundschule

I hadn't seen her for three years because we'd ended up going to different schools and I'd **moved** to another part of town. It was great to see her again – here of all places. I immediately started to push my way through to the other side. I was so thrilled about my discovery that I hardly heard the casting begin. The first girls came up onto the catwalk and stuttered something about themselves. One of them was so nervous she even forgot her own name. Then things **gradually** got better and the applicants began to relax a bit. As I made my way across to Debbie I was astounded to hear that some of the girls already had modelling experience and some had even been amongst the finalists in beauty competitions. Well, they were welcome to it. For me the only important thing right now was seeing Debbie again.

I finally managed to get to her. She still had her back turned to me. I quietly **crept** up to her from behind and put my hands over her eyes. Before I could say "surprise!" she screamed really loud and **spun around**. I immediately dropped my hands. My God, the girl was **jumpy**. But then I suddenly remembered that she had a phobia against **blind man's buff**. Too late. The presentation on the catwalk came to a temporary halt and everybody stared at us. I wanted the ground to open up and swallow me!

"Kiki," **squealed** Debbie as she recognised me. That

---

to move – umziehen; gradually – allmählich;
to creep – schleichen; to spin around – sich rasch umdrehen;
jumpy – schreckhaft; blind man's buff – Blindekuh;
to squeal – kreischen

only made things even more embarrassing for me because my name was now **on record** as a **troublemaker**. Well, that was it for me! They surely wouldn't let me participate in the fashion show now – not after making such a negative impression.

Fortunately, the Centre Manager just made some **witty** comment after what seemed to me was an **eternity** of silence, and the casting continued.

I pulled Debbie behind a **partition** with a huge advertising poster from Mum's agency on it. There we gave each other a hug, despite the stress, and gave each other a few kisses just like in old times.

She was as thrilled as I was that we'd both been invited to the casting. It was an act of fate, there was no question about it. So we both decided that we would definitely get through the casting round and then take part in the fashion show together.

"That'll be fantastic," I whispered to her. "You and me, we always were an **unbeatable** team!"

Life is a **steady-flowing river**. Some philosopher said that. He probably didn't know anything about life because he lived in some cave or **barrel** or on some desert island and did nothing but talk to himself all day long. Whatever. One thing's for sure: he didn't know anything about *my* life, otherwise he wouldn't have come up with

---

on record – aktenkundig; troublemaker – Störenfried;
witty – launig; eternity – Ewigkeit; partition – Stellwand;
unbeatable – unschlagbar; steady-flowing river – ruhiger Fluss;
barrel – Tonne

a theory like that. If my life had any similarity with a river, then it was more like a mountain stream which **hurtled** over **rapids** into the valley.

I couldn't help thinking this was definitely the case when I came out from behind the partition with Debbie and turned my attention back to the catwalk. It wasn't my **turn** for quite a while because I was at the end of the alphabet, but now that Debbie and I both wanted to be chosen, I looked at the competition with a lot more interest.

A seventeen-year-old brunette with strangely **curly** hair was just introducing herself. She looked a bit **drab** and had a rather large **bum**. I was surprised to hear that she'd won "Face of the Month" in a magazine for young people and even been "Miss-Morning-Queen" on a TV channel. They obviously hadn't looked **properly**.

"Isn't that the channel where they do bikini films?" I asked Debbie.

Debbie nodded.

No thank you, I thought. I wouldn't put myself on show in a swimming costume with a bum like that. And leaving the bum to one side, I wouldn't do it **out of principle** anyway.

A blonde horse came onto the catwalk. I thought that even before she opened her mouth to introduce herself. But when she talked, her lower jaw **ground** so **promi-**

---

to hurtle – sausen; rapids – Stromschnellen;
to be one's turn – dran sein; curly – gelockt; drab – farblos;
bum – Hintern; properly – richtig; out of principle – aus Prinzip;
to grind – mahlen; prominently – auffallend

**nently**, I couldn't help but think of a **hay**-chewing horse. The girl's movements were strangely **awkward**, probably because she was so **heavily built**. She was at least 1.90 m tall and I couldn't imagine that it was too easy for her to find clothes which fitted her in the boutiques in the City-Centre.

"They won't pick her, that's for sure," I whispered to Debbie.

"No," she replied, shaking her head. But then she nodded to the catwalk and said with **a look of acknowledgement**, "But they'll take *her* for sure."

I was still **engrossed** with the horse who – for some reason – absolutely fascinated me, but I then looked in the same direction as Debbie and had to grab her arm to stop myself from fainting.

On the catwalk in front of us – with a confident stride and swinging hips – was none other than Mona, strolling up to the jury's table with self-assurance and a beaming smile.

Make her **twist her ankle** or fall off the catwalk, I begged fate with a pounding heart. Whatever! Just do something to stop her from taking part in the fashion show. Because the fact that the jury would choose her was **as sure as eggs are eggs**.

"My name is Mona Martens," she said into the mi-

---

hay – Heu; awkward – kantig; heavily built – kräftig gebaut;
a look of acknowledgement – anerkennender Blick;
engrossed – vertieft;
to twist one's ankle – mit dem Fuß umknicken;
as sure as eggs are eggs – so sicher wie das Amen in der Kirche

crophone as if she'd been working professionally as a **presenter** for years. "I'm thirteen years old and would really like to take part in the fashion show. I take ballet classes and love music, so I don't think I'll have a problem learning the choreography. Besides, I like working in a team and I'm easy to get on with."

I love music!! Tzzzzz. Didn't she say that she was completely **unmusical** and that's why she had to go to the Art study-group? And easy to get on with? What a **deceitful** cow!!!

"Where are the toilets, Debbie?" I whispered. "I think I'm going to **puke**."

Debbie looked at me **anxiously**. "Are you feeling ill?"

"Aren't you?"

"No, why?"

I considered letting her know the truth about Mona Martens, but then I decided to wait. If we were both chosen, there'd be plenty of time to do that.

But it looked like they were probably only going to pick one girl from our age group. And, of course, they'd probably already decided for Mona even before we crept up onto the catwalk.

"Do you think they'll take any other teenies apart from Mona?" I asked with my usual pessimism.

"Of course, they will. They need three or four for each group, otherwise they'll hardly be able to present anything."

I had no idea about how the fashion show was going to

---

presenter – Moderator; unmusical – unmusikalisch;
deceitful – hinterlistig; to puke – kotzen; anxiously – besorgt

be structured, so I tried to get a grip on myself and be a **calculated optimist**.

And when, after four other girls – all of whom weren't bad at all – Mona's appearance gradually began **to fade** from my inner eye, I slowly began to give us a chance again. After all, we were completely different. I loved music, too, and we'd soon see if my jazz dance group came across better than her ballet.

My self-confidence had managed to regain some stability by the time my name was called.

I was glad I hadn't put on a tight skirt but was wearing **comfy** trousers and a top. I felt comfortable in my clothes and thanks to my sporty shoes I didn't break my leg like a number of other **contestants** as they clambered up onto the catwalk.

As I went up the steps, I found myself looking at Mona. I was **briefly** puzzled: hadn't she just smiled at me? That really was the height of arrogance. In a flash I was as cool as a cucumber. Just you wait, girl, I thought, you'll be **laughing on the other side of your face**. I slipped my right hand casually in my trouser pocket and stepped towards the jury table, humming a song from the charts to myself. I did a **spin** in front of the jury – just like I'd practised dozens of times in the jazz dance group – smiled my most radiant toothpaste smile, took a few steps back, made another turn and stopped with a smile

---

calculated optimism – Zweckoptimist; to fade – verblassen;
comfy – bequem; contestant – Wettbewerbsteilnehmer;
briefly – kurz; sb will be laughing on the other side of one's face – jmdm. wird das Lachen noch vergehen; spin – Drehung

in front of the microphone. Just like Mona, I took the microphone off the stand – it looked much cooler like that – and casually held it up to my mouth.

Yes, and then it happened: I had no idea what to say. I completely **dried up**. In front of all those people staring at me!

This isn't really happening, I thought. Some comedian or other who writes for stupid sitcoms has just thought this up. Things like this don't happen in reality! **So much for** life being a steady-flowing river. Once again the stream of my life **lashed** against the rapids. My tranquil waters swirled up into a **foaming spray**.

I looked up for help, and my gaze fell upon a familiar face. Mum! Crikey, I'd completely forgotten about her. She was standing there on the gallery with all her team. I couldn't **disgrace** her like this. What was she doing now? She gave me the thumbs up, and all the people standing around her did the same.

I suddenly felt really happy that they were **backing** me and were counting on my success. I found my voice again.

"Excuse me," I said, turning slightly red. "When you're up here, you feel a bit gobsmacked. But at least I haven't forgotten my name."

The audience laughed at this **allusion** to my **predecessor** and a few of the jury members smiled to themselves.

---

to dry up – stecken bleiben; so much for … – von wegen …;
to lash – peitschen; foaming spray – schäumende Gischt;
to disgrace – blamieren; to back sb – jmdm. den Rücken stärken;
allusion – Anspielung; predecessor – Vorgänger

"My name's Kristina. I'm thirteen years old and that's how I feel."

Laughter again.

"I've never taken part in a fashion show before, and I have absolutely no idea how it all works, but I imagine it's pretty good fun. Because of the music as well. I'm a **passionate** member of a jazz dance group."

I smiled over to the jury table because I was slowly running out of things to say. I'd said enough really. I was here to exhibit fashion items, not **waffle** on forever.

So I decided to throw in a quick final comment. "My mum says I look like the proverbial girl next door," I said. "So if you're looking for something in that direction, then just give me a call."

Oh, for crying out loud, that sounded absolutely **awful**! How could I come up with a load of rubbish like that? It was all because of what Mum had said. On the other hand, maybe it was exactly what they were looking for. I put the microphone back onto the stand, tried to give the jury a **captivating** smile and strolled back to the steps. Once there I turned around again. I was curious to see how the jury members responded to my exit. They were all looking at me and, as I smiled, they started to applaud.

They'd done that with all the other contestants as well, but I got it into my head that the applause was louder this time.

Debbie obviously thought the same because she was smiling from one ear to the other. "Fantastic!" she said

---

passionate – leidenschaftlich; to waffle – schwafeln;
awful – schrecklich; captivating – gewinnend

full of enthusiasm. "You were just great. No one would believe you'd never been on a catwalk before. You **took** the jury **by storm**. If they don't pick you, then I have no idea what they're looking for!"

They picked me. And Debbie, too. They chose exactly twelve female and two male models. And, of course, they took Mona as well. Grrr!

Needless to say, Mum was completely **beside herself** and my brother, too. As they came down the **escalator** after the official end of the casting and the announcement of the winners, the Joker came running up to me like he was on fire. He hugged me and kissed me so much he **scared the living daylights out of** me.

"You're great, Kiki, fabulous, groovy, far out ..." He almost fell over himself with **praise**. I would never have thought that he'd show such **heartfelt** interest in my fate and be so thrilled by my success.

"Stop, stop!" I had to push him off after a while because I wanted to say goodbye properly to Debbie. Without her encouraging presence I would probably have **bungled** the whole thing.

"Let's call when we get the invitation to the choreography sessions. We can meet up beforehand for an ice-cream." We quickly exchanged mobile phone numbers

---

to take sth by storm – etwas im Sturm erobern;
to be beside oneself – aus dem Häuschen sein;
escalator – Rolltreppe; to scare the living daylights out of sb – jmdn. zu Tode erschrecken;
praise – Lob; heartfelt – innig; to bungle – vergeigen

and then Debbie ran to her parents who had apparently been waiting for her the whole time in front of the City-Centre. They were really **proud** of their daughter.

Mum and the Joker were also **full of go**, and so it was OK that we went to the Mexican restaurant to eat chicken wings. That made it a four-star day for my brother.

His way of classifying everything in stars was his latest **quirk**. He'd picked it up during our last holiday in Mallorca, and he used it for more than just **evaluating** hotels. Three-star ice-cream – pretty tasty. Five-star movie in the cinema – bombastic. And a one-star sister – really stupid! They'd all come up.

But like I said, the day of my casting was a really great four-star day, and I couldn't help but agree with this **judgement** as I **munched** away at my chicken wings.

The travel bag and the laptop in the hall **gave it away**: Dad was home.

"What brings you to us in the middle of the week?" I asked him **taken aback**. "No parliamentary session at the moment?"

He gave me a quick, friendly hug. "It's the **election campaign**! You know, the local government elections. I have to show myself in my **constituency** and support the local candidates from the national party."

---

proud – stolz; to be full of go – aufgedreht sein;
quirk – Marotte; to evaluate – bewerten;
judgement – Beurteilung; to munch – knabbern;
to give away sth – etwas verraten; taken aback – erstaunt;
election campaign – Wahlkampf; constituency – Wahlkreis

"Oh," mumbled the Joker disappointed. "So you're just here to work. And I thought I'd get to see you as well."

He didn't always cope very well with the fact that Dad was often away from home for weeks on end and he could only communicate with him via mobile phone or internet. That meant, of course, it wasn't possible to play football with him, which is what the fathers of all his friends did almost every evening after work. Dad had a really guilty conscience about this and so it was hardly surprising that he immediately made the Joker an offer.

"Well, I'm sure we can get a game of football in while I'm here."

But the Joker remained sceptical. Dad's promises and plans had so often fallen through because of **urgent** meetings called at **short notice**. "I'll believe that when we set off with a ball under our arm," he said.

Mum helped Dad out. "It'll work out."

She **rummaged** around in the fridge and conjured up a late-night snack for Dad on the table.

Dad – who **incidentally** had pretty dark rings under his eyes and looked really exhausted – threw himself at the food **with** considerable **relish**.

It goes without saying that I immediately told him about my casting success. But instead of reacting with enthusiasm as I had expected, he had lots of reservations. When he heard that Mum had started the whole thing off, he even started to get angry.

---

urgent – dringend; short notice – kurzfristig;
to rummage – durchwühlen; incidentally – übrigens;
with relish – mit Behagen

"How could you **entice** Kiki to do something like that?" he said critically. "I don't want my daughter **putting** herself **on display** in public."

I beg your pardon? That was an argument from the Middle Ages! And my reaction to this didn't exactly come as a surprise. "What's that supposed to mean?! As a politician you're constantly putting yourself on display to the public. What's the difference between my fashion show and your election campaign?"

"There's no comparison. I'm not a pretty young girl, and men don't stare at me **lasciviously**."

Now he really wasn't feeling well at all! I wanted to go on the catwalk, not **on the game**! I was so **outraged** my voice started to get louder. "Get a grip, Dad! The fashion show audience aren't all **lechers**!"

Mum **butted in**. "Don't use that tone of voice with your father, Kristina!" she warned me, although I was sure she agreed with me **on the content**. When she called me Kristina, she usually meant business.

"I don't want you to talk to your father like one of your mates from the schoolyard. He's a figure of respect."

Oh, they were both **resorting to** some of the best philosophical aspects of the Middle Ages in this discussion! A figure of respect?! Tzzzz. Pull out the **rod of authority**

---

to entice – verleiten; to put on display – zur Schau stellen;
lasciviously – lüstern; on the game – auf den Strich;
outraged – empört; lecher – Lustmolch;
to butt in – sich einmischen; on the content – inhaltlich;
to resort to sth – zurückgreifen auf etwas;
rod of authority – die autoritäre Rute

and wave it around a bit **threateningly**, why not? Crikey people, I thought, give me a break, will you. I mean, your children have turned out pretty well, haven't they?

But as far as **manners** were concerned, Mum was rather conservative and she was surprisingly allergic to disrespectful and **discourteous** expressions.

"You can use that kind of language when you're with your friends, but in this house people will speak in a way which shows respect for the person they're talking to."

First of all we had a debate about the meaning and meaninglessness of fashion shows, all the **hullabaloo** about fashion and the bad influence an event like this could have on my still **spotless** soul.

"They'll put crazy ideas into Kristina's head. She'll start having completely unrealistic dreams of a career on the catwalk."

"But Dad," I tried to reassure him, "it's just a bit of harmless fun. A cool experience. What did Grandad always say: every now and again you have to do something really exciting to keep going in life. That was his motto."

Mum smiled to herself, the Joker grinned cheekily and Dad was **in a tight corner**.

"Of course, you should do something unusual now and again, but it doesn't have to be this modelling rubbish, does it?" Bit by bit he seemed to be giving up, and in the end he resigned himself to **the inevitable**.

---

threateningly – drohend; manners – Umgangsformen; discourteous – unhöflich; hullabaloo – Trara; spotless – makellos; in a tight corner – in der Klemme; the inevitable – das Unvermeidliche

"When you two decide things like this next time, I want to be asked first," he said grumpily.

"Yes, sure, we already did, but we couldn't reach you," I **conceded**.

I couldn't help thinking that Dad hadn't asked us when he gave up his managerial job to go into politics. What did he care about how we found all the election-campaign posters around town showing him with a big grin on his face? I mean, he didn't have to hear all those stupid comments in school because of that. And he didn't have the Joker come running up to him in the middle of break, crying his eyes out because some boy from his year had said it was Dad's fault that the city was **broke** and that the school didn't have enough teachers and that our classrooms couldn't be painted.

"Rubbish," I'd said in Dad's defence. "Dad hasn't got anything to do with the town. He does **national politics**."

But I don't think the Joker really understood the difference and so it didn't help much. Electoral campaigns were really **tough going** for the children of politicians.

Before I went to sleep, I had to call Franzi again.

"Are you off your rocker?" she groaned sleepily. "It's midnight and we've got school tomorrow!"

"Oh, sorry. I didn't see the time. You can't believe how exciting it all was today ..."

"Hmmm." She didn't exactly let herself get **carried away**.

---

to concede – einlenken; broke – pleite; national politics – Bundespolitik; tough going – die Härte; to carry away – mitreißen

"Just imagine! They actually picked me!"

"Yeah, congratulations, can I go back to sleep now?"

I had really expected a bit more enthusiasm from my best friend. After she'd been sent away from the City-Centre early, I thought she would be really curious to hear my report.

"Really?" she said in reply to my complaint, "but I was already asleep. Tell me about it tomorrow in detail over a coffee, OK?"

That wasn't enough to satisfy my need to talk, but it was a **reasonable** offer.

"OK," I agreed. "But keep it to yourself. I don't want the *Pepper Dollies* **spreading** it around school."

She promised her complete discretion and went back to bed with another **yawn**.

As I started to feel the **strain** of the day as well, I did the same.

I turned off the light and closed my eyes. The last person I thought about before falling asleep was Meik. He'd be amazed when I walked up to him in the schoolyard the next time – because I'd be walking like a model. He wouldn't deny me to his mates a second time!

It was really annoying that Mona was also taking part in the fashion show, but I **swore** not to let her outstrip me – either at the show or with Meik. No way!

---

reasonable – vernünftig; to spread – verbreiten;
yawn – Gähnen; strain – Anspannung; to swear – schwören

# Kiki's had enough

Because of the casting the evening before I hadn't paid much attention to my homework, and in German first thing in the morning my thoughts kept wandering back to the fashion show and to Meik. I would soon pay the price for my lack of concentration.

"Get your homework out!" Wölfchen commanded, and he marched down the aisles to check everyone had done their homework.

Before I knew it, he was standing behind me. He glanced at the **double spread** of my exercise book and said **curtly**, "So? What's the problem?"

I was still lost in my thoughts about Meik. "What problem?" I asked startled and disoriented, "I don't have a problem. At least, not one that you could solve."

The boys snorted with laughter.

"I see ... your homework is not complete and you're cheeky **to boot**. Points off for that."

Disgruntled, he went to find his next victim.

I didn't know what was going on.

"What's the matter with him?" I whispered over to

---

double spread – Doppelseite; curtly – unwirsch;
to boot – obendrein

Franzi. "He should be happy to hear I don't have a problem."

Franzi grinned. "Come on, Kiki! After the **summary** we were meant to write a short problem profile for the story. That's what he meant. Not if *you* have a problem."

Oh, that's what they call a **Freudian slip** – I was obviously so stressed that I'd overlooked this specific problem for all my own problems.

"Do you think I'm going to get a bad **mark** now?" I asked Franzi anxiously in the morning break. After all, German was one of the highlights in my school **report**.

"It won't be all that bad. You'll just have to make sure you do your homework properly for a while. Then everything will be fine."

In the next lesson we had Geography, and I was quite sure that Wölfchen would now **grill** me. Unfortunately, Geography was a subject that remained a mystery to me despite all the years I'd been doing it in school.

As far as my globe was concerned, it was full of white **patches** – more and more unexplored terrain. Regrettably Wölfchen showed no **consideration** for this.

"At a time of globalisation," he said, "it's increasingly important that you can find the way not just out of your front door and back, but throughout the world. Kristina, you happy girl without problems, could you please tell me the capital of Malaysia?"

---

summary – Zusammenfassung;
Freudian slip – freudsche Fehlleistung; mark – Note;
report – Zeugnis; to grill sb – jmdm. auf den Zahn fühlen;
patch – Fleck; consideration – Rücksicht

I didn't miss the slightly **smug** undertone of his question, and I would have liked to give him the right answer, but, unfortunately, Malaysia was located in one of those white patches I just mentioned. Huh?

I looked over to Greetje for help. She was **ace** at Geography. She **mouthed** a word to me, but reading people's lips really wasn't my strong point and I remained just as much in the dark.

"Well? I'm waiting!"

Wölfchen was getting **impatient** and a few boys started giggling.

I have no idea what came over me. I expect the arrogant grin on Mona's face just got on my nerves. I suddenly felt the need to say something – anything – just so I wasn't sitting there looking like an idiot. What I then said **slipped out** of me spontaneously: "Could you give me a choice of four or can I ask the audience?"

The laughter after this allusion to quiz shows was **indescribable**, and even the **hint** of a smile darted over Wölfchen's face. Well then, I'd managed to get out of that pretty well. At least I thought so at the time.

"OK then, let's ask the audience." Wölfchen went along with the game. "Who knows the answer?"

I could have strangled her as Mona put her hand up.

"Kuala Lumpur," she said in an extremely casual tone of voice. "Bit of a **waste** of a lifeline in my opinion. That was only a two-thousand-Euro question."

---

smug – süffisant; ace – Ass; to mouth sth – etwas lautlos sagen; impatient – ungeduldig; to slip out – herausrutschen; indescribable – unbeschreiblich; hint – Hauch; waste – Verschwendung

She now had the laughter on her side and, because she'd also given the right answer, Wölfchen laughed openly as well. I'd been **taken for a ride** yet again. Grrr!

I wasn't just happy when school was over because of the stupid episode in Geography, I was dead tired and had just had enough. And when our history teacher, Mr Birkenstock, made some comment about how my father was a politician so I should know what the job of the Lower House of Parliament in Germany was, that was the limit.

"It's my father who sits in parliament, not me!" I said **stroppily**. "I'm sure he'd be able to tell the class about it." And on an impulse of pure **folly** I added, "Talk to him about it!"

But my sarcasm **backfired**.

"That's a great idea!" Birkenstock almost jumped out of his ecologically friendly sandals with delight. "That would be fantastic – a genuine **enrichment** of our lesson. Could you ask him?"

NOOOOO! I could have screamed. As far as I was concerned, I didn't want my dad poking his nose around my school, let alone around my class. He'd just make a fool of me.

"Er, yeah, of course, no problem ..." I stuttered. "I can ask him, but he's really busy right now because of the election campaign."

And I really hoped he would turn me down. That's all

---

to take sb for a ride – jmdn. anschmieren; stroppy – pampig; folly – Schwachsinn; to backfire – nach hinten losgehen; enrichment – Bereicherung

I needed now: after Mona's stupid comments, more stupid comments about my dad.

In the bus I asked myself where Meik had got to because, as much as I tried to **dislocate** my neck in the main break, I couldn't see him anywhere. Hm, I'd have **to get to the bottom of** this. I couldn't let the guy slip through my fingers and start something with Mona!

If I'd hoped to go home and relax and dedicate all my thoughts to Meik until meeting up with Franzi for a coffee, I was very much **mistaken**. Instead of being met by peace and quiet, I was greeted by **pandemonium**.

"Bloody hell, where have you been?" the Joker snapped at me before I'd even taken my rucksack off. "Dad's got his **election rally**. Don't you want to come with us?"

Not really, no. What was the point standing around in a huge crowd? I knew what he was going to say **off by heart**. On the other hand this was about an act of family solidarity, and it wouldn't have been very nice if I just **bottled out**, especially as Dad had to leave in the morning. So I cancelled the coffee with Franzi and said I would join them. The things I did for harmony in the family!

---

to dislocate – verrenken;
to get to the bottom of sth – einer Sache auf den Grund gehen;
to be mistaken – sich täuschen; pandemonium – Chaos;
election rally – Wahlkundgebung; off by heart – auswendig;
to bottle out – kneifen

Dad was picked up by the campaign bus and we were allowed to go with him. It was always a strange feeling for me to see Dad with his party friends. Sure, he was my dad, he didn't **put on an act**, but it was almost as if he had just got changed from wearing a **tracksuit** to a fine **dinner jacket**. It **gave me the creeps** a bit the way he slipped from one role into the other. What would happen if he couldn't change back? But Mum said all politicians were a little bit the actor, and actors never had a problem going back to being themselves after each performance.

"You have to look at it like this," Dad had once explained to me. "Life is a **stage**, and there's a front stage and a backstage. All the official things go on front stage – the public life – but backstage is reserved for private life. You can let your hair down there and do all the things with your friends that are **frowned upon** in public."

The truth was it wasn't any different in school. Most of us made an effort to behave properly in the classroom and when a teacher was around, but as soon as we were in the schoolyard, the **sexual innuendoes** started, people smoked in secret, there was suppressed and open aggression to one another and a lot of **bad language**. The schoolyard was just another stage with another distribution of roles. Guys **set the tone** there who never even opened

---

to put on an act – sich verstellen; tracksuit – Trainingsanzug;
dinner jacket – Smoking;
sth gives sb the creeps – etwas ist jmdm. unheimlich;
stage – Bühne; frowned upon – verpönt;
sexual innuendoes – sexuelle Anspielungen;
bad language – Schimpfwörter; to set the tone – den Ton angeben

their mouths during lesson time, and the biggest losers in the classroom were often the **big shots** in the schoolyard.

I was still brooding over this strange phenomenon as we got to the market square and Dad dragged us onto the "front stage" so he could **pose** with his family in front of the press before making his big speech.

No, how embarrassing. If I'd have known he was going to do that – give or take solidarity – I would have stayed at home.

I managed to make my escape after the first round of photos and, mumbling an apology, I slipped away to the **archways** of the old **town hall**, where I hid myself from the gaze of the curious voters behind a pillar.

Feeling rather groggy, I leaned against the cold sandstone and closed my eyes for a moment.

"Feeling **weary**?" someone suddenly asked from next to me. I couldn't place the voice at first. "I didn't know you had connections to Siebert!"

Oh, no! I tore open my eyes and found myself looking right into Meik's face.

"He's my father," I admitted **tentatively**.

"Your father? The **Member of Parliament**?"

He fell silent for a moment, probably to let the information sink in. I guess it was a shock for him to hear that I was the daughter of a Member of Parliament.

But he seemed to be full of **compassion** rather than

---

big shot – hohes Tier; to pose – posieren; archway – Arkade; town hall – Rathaus; weary – erschöpft; tentatively – zögerlich; Member of Parliament – Bundestagsabgeordneter; compassion – Mitleid

awe. "It must be pretty stressful being the daughter of a politician, isn't it? Having the press around all the time and all the **hassle**!"

You could say that again. Give me a break, stress! And now Meik turns up **out of the blue**. Where did he come from?

"What ... what are you doing here?" I stuttered, still taken aback and my nerves all over the place.

"Just keeping myself informed. I can vote for the first time at this election."

That means he's already sixteen, I thought. My God, three years older than me. He'll never be interested in me.

But **oddly enough** he seemed to be just that. Probably just because I was the daughter of a politician. That even gave a "girl next door" a slightly interesting aura. Well, whatever. At least it was a starting-point and, besides, it wasn't exactly a bad situation, just the two of us. Better than in the schoolyard where people kept making dirty comments about us.

But then the speeches began and I didn't have the problem of having to start a deep or **witty** conversation with him.

All of a sudden, I thought the election campaign was great. What a wonderful situation I was in. The crowd was forcing him to **squeeze up** next to me. I could feel his breath on my neck, and my back was almost touching his

---

hassle – Theater; out of the blue – aus heiterem Himmel;
oddly enough – seltsamerweise; witty – geistreich, witzig;
to squeeze up – einquetschen

chest. Why just "almost"? *Let yourself go, girl,* my inner voice called to me. *Go on. You won't get an opportunity like this again soon.* I was a bit embarrassed at the thought, but the **temptation** was too great. As a corpulent woman pushed her big bum into my stomach, I took advantage of the situation to lean against him. I was **trembling** inside, but he didn't **back off**. I asked myself whether it was because he didn't want to or because he couldn't because of the crowd. But who cares?! It was utterly **irrelevant**. I was close to him – so incredibly close – in a way I would never have got close to him in the schoolyard. That was all that counted. When I tell the *Pepper Dollies* about this tomorrow! I could hardly believe my sudden luck. I'd like to see Mona get this far! *Maybe she already has got this far,* said the little **killjoy** in my head, *school buses are sometimes really full as well. Maybe she squeezes up to him every morning.* A **drop of bitterness** trickled down my **gullet**. I **cleared my throat** and tried to get rid of the horrible taste, but jealousy had cast its shadow over this wonderful moment.

As the rally came to an end and the crowd slowly **dispersed**, Mum came rushing up to me with the Joker. When she spotted Meik next to me and saw me leaning against him **for no apparent reason**, she immediately got that Oh-you've-got-a-boyfriend-and-don't-you-want-

---

temptation – Versuchung; to tremble – zittern;
to back off – zurückweichen; irrelevant – unerheblich;
killjoy – Miesmacher; drop of bitterness – Wermutstropfen;
gullet – Speiseröhre; to clear one's throat – sich räuspern;
to disperse – zerstreuen; for no apparent reason – völlig grundlos

to-introduce-him-to-me-look in her eyes. Well, no I didn't. First of all, he wasn't my boyfriend yet, and secondly, it had nothing to do with her. I gave her a warning look. She got the message and **reigned in** her curiosity. But she started to lead us over to a **stall** where we could eat something.

"You can come, too," said the Joker to Meik as he noticed him hesitate. "We get the hot dogs for free."

It didn't occur to him, of course, that Meik might have other reasons than economic ones not to subject himself to my **gathered** family clan.

"What's your name?" the Joker continued to **pester** Meik.

"Meik. He's called Meik," I answered **irritably** and Meik looked at me in surprise, probably wondering how I knew his name. I smiled to myself and decided to tell him later maybe. Later, when things developed between us, as I hoped. We went and got a hot dog and stood to eat them at a table to one side – which the Joker didn't think was so good.

"There's enough space here," he said, and I had to give him a kick in the **shins** before he understood that I wanted to be alone with Meik.

"Alright, alright. I get the message!" he said, looking at me all upset. "You don't have to get so **heavy-handed**!"

I got us a Coke and when I put the paper cups on the

---

to reign in – bezähmen; stall – Stand, Imbissbude;
gathered – versammelt; to pester – löchern; irritably – genervt;
shin – Schienbein; heavy-handed – handgreiflich

table, I couldn't **resist** alluding to the stupid situation in front of the drinks dispenser.

"It looks like I can manage to get the drinks today without your help."

He looked a bit embarrassed, which I was pleased to see because he obviously knew perfectly well that he hadn't exactly been nice to me a few days ago.

"I'm sorry about that," he said. "It was a stupid situation. I just didn't want them to make any more stupid comments. But it probably wasn't the best idea to **get rid of** them."

"No, it wasn't at all," I said. "I was pretty angry about it. No boy has ever made a fool of me like that. As if I couldn't even get a Coke out of the drinks dispenser!"

Even thinking about the situation made me feel **livid** again.

"You could have said something," he said with a grin. "You don't seem to have a **shortage** in the temperament **department**."

What was that supposed to mean? I stared at him.

"Oh don't look so **grim**. I'll make it up to you. Come on, let's go and eat an ice-cream for dessert. It's on me."

**Cymbals** and **harps** couldn't have been more pleasant to my ears than those words. I couldn't believe it. Could it really be that Meik – who I had already almost given up on – was inviting me for an ice-cream?

"What's the matter? Isn't that enough?"

---

to resist – widerstehen; to get rid of sb – abwimmeln;
livid – stinksauer; shortage – Mangel; department – Abteilung;
grim – finster; cymbal – Zimbel; harp – Harfe

I saw him through a cloud of pink which had **enveloped** me and I didn't understand anything anymore.

"Or don't you have time right now?"

Did I have time right now? Of course, I had time. All the time in the world because someone's powerful hand had just stopped the earth from turning and had paused the **pulsating** of the universe.

"Who cares about time," I said, feeling completely **dazed**.

"We can philosophise about that in the **ice-cream parlour**," he said with a grin. He'd obviously spotted that I was completely beside myself. He pushed me **gently** in the direction of the City-Centre.

"Come on, let's go to Coko. They've got the best ice-cream there."

And, because all I could do was to agree with him, we set off to Coko.

On the way my mobile phone suddenly started to ring.

"Yes?"

It was the Joker.

"Mum wants to know if you're coming back with us. We want to go in a minute."

I looked at Meik. "Should I go back with the campaign bus? Right now?"

He shook his head.

"No. Tell Mum I'll come home later. We're going for an ice-cream."

Meik grinned. "Listen," he said, looking at the mobile

---

to envelop – einhüllen; to pulsate – pulsieren; dazed – benebelt; ice-cream parlour – Eisdiele; gently – sanft

phone in my hand. "Would you give me your mobile phone number?"

"Sure. Why not?"

Someone who you went to eat ice-cream with could have it any time, even if Franzi always warned: "Never give a boy your mobile phone number. It's so annoying."

I have no idea where she formed her opinion from. As far as I could see, she didn't have any boys who could be annoying in her life – with or without mobile phones. With the exception of Raffi.

We stopped and exchanged telephone numbers.

"What name should I save your number under?" asked Meik. "Siebert is a bit **impersonal**. And Juliet … well, it's a bit **over-used**."

I giggled. It was about time he took some interest in my name.

"OK, then write Kiki. That's what my friends call me. My real name is Kristina."

He typed in my name with a smile. "Kiki is good. It sounds cheeky."

"You like cheeky girls?"

"Yeah, the cheekier, the better."

Aha, then he'd like Mona as well.

As soon as this thought came into my head, I got annoyed about it.

Either Mona had suddenly come between us in the form of a nasty ghost or the ice-cream had cooled down our feelings, but for some reason the easy-going mood we'd had in the market square had disappeared in a

---

impersonal – unpersönlich; over-used – abgenutzt

flash. Everything felt really **stiff** and frosty in the ice-cream parlour, all of a sudden. First of all, I couldn't decide which ice-cream I wanted because everything was pretty expensive and I didn't want to take advantage of him. And then, when I finally decided on the **cracknel tumbler**, Miss Embarrassment sat down at our table as an **uninvited** guest and suffocated every attempt at conversation. We **spooned** the ice-cream into our mouths in silence, hardly daring to look at each other under Miss Embarrassment's strict gaze. In the end, I couldn't bear it anymore. Get lost, Miss Embarrassment, you're not welcome here! But she just laughed cynically and, like the evil witch in **Sleeping Beauty**, she fell silent just like us.

When Meik suddenly said something to me out of the blue, I was so startled that I knocked over the ice-cream tumbler with an uncontrolled movement and the chocolate sauce, ice-cream and splinters of cracknel spilled over the table and onto his beige trousers.

I threw my hands up to my face in horror. I just couldn't bear the sight of my **mishap**. "Oh no, what have I done?" I stuttered.

And at the same time I thought: it's over, you can forget about him, he now thinks you're a **danger to the public**, he'll **steer well clear of** you in the future.

---

stiff – steif; cracknel tumbler – Krokantbecher;
uninvited – ungebeten; to spoon – löffeln;
Sleeping Beauty – Dornröschen; mishap – Malheur;
danger to the public – gemeingefährlich;
to steer well clear of sb – einen Bogen um jmdn. machen

But I pulled myself together, grabbed the tiny paper napkin lying on the table, leaned over to him and tried to clean his trousers. Needless to say, that only made things even more embarrassing.

He pushed me back gently.

"It's OK, I'll do that. It's no big deal."

No big deal?! Did he just **miss** what had happened? I'd just completely ruined his trousers and he didn't think it was such a big deal! Cripes, the boy was the personification of gentleness. He **dabbed** around at his trousers a bit and then he stood up.

"I'm going to the toilet to wash it off," he said, and his voice sounded reasonably **calm**.

Man, he was a **master** of self-control. If I were him, I would **have had a go at** me straightaway: can't you be a bit more careful, you silly cow? Yeah, well, he probably thought that anyway. He was just too **well brought up** to say it.

I jumped up as well. "I'll come with you to help!"

He **gave a wry smile**. "No, it's OK, I'll manage myself ..."

As soon as he stood up, I was horrified to see exactly where the ice-cream had landed: there was no way I could help him clean that delicate part of his trousers. And the men's toilet wasn't exactly the right place for me either! A hot flush went through my whole body. My hands

---

to miss – verpassen; to dab – tupfen; calm – gefasst;
master – Meister; to have a go at sb – jmdn. anschnauzen;
well brought up – wohl erzogen;
to give a wry smile – schief grinsen

were really sweaty all of a sudden. I wanted the ground to swallow me up.

The giggling and silly comments from the next table only **confirmed** my feeling that I'd completely **messed** things **up** yet again.

And the worst thing of all was that Mona would squeeze up to him in the crowded school bus the next morning and he would think about this awful experience with me and find her even more attractive. I mean, who wants to have a girlfriend who throws ice-cream tumblers over you in public?

"I don't believe it!" Franzi was **knocked for six** when I called her that evening. "You went for an ice-cream with him?" Ice-cream-throwing would have been the more accurate description. "Well, I never! You **lucky devil**!"

A devil maybe, but lucky? I certainly wasn't both. Just the ice-cream devil.

Without hearing about the more intimate details of the evening, Franzi gave her opinion about the **course** I should take: "**Stick with** him. You really have to stick with him now."

For a moment I thought about telling her about my mishap, but then I decided it was better not to. Even a best friend didn't have to hear every embarrassing detail.

But with her **inimitable** instinct for human emotions,

---

to confirm – bestätigen; to mess up – versagen;
to be knocked for six – von den Socken sein;
lucky devil – Glückskind; course – Kurs;
to stick with sb – dranbleiben; inimitable – unnachahmlich

Franzi had already **sensed** that something wasn't quite right with me.

"You don't sound particularly happy," she said. "Where's the problem? Don't you think he's serious about it?"

Wow, she didn't beat about the bush. But how was I meant to know the answer after only one date? Theoretically I didn't even know if I was serious about it myself. And after all that had happened in the ice-cream parlour ... no!

"It's too early to say."

"But you must have a feeling about whether it could turn into a relationship or not! You must feel something."

I refused to talk about it. After what had happened, nothing could come out of it, **least of all** a relationship. A little tear of regret and **self-pity** trickled down my cheek. Oh, what the hell, I thought, the frustration just had to come out. And so I told Franzi everything.

"Hasn't he got a sense of humour?" she asked. "The situation sounds pretty funny to me."

"Yeah, but you didn't get the tumbler of ice-cream over your trousers."

"Was he really angry? How did it end?"

The scene of horror was still vivid in my memory.

"Well, he came out of the toilet with a wet patch over his you-know-what. It looked like he'd **peed** in his pants."

---

to sense – spüren;
least of all – am wenigsten; self-pity – Selbstmitleid;
to pee – pinkeln

Franzi giggled.

"It wasn't funny at all," I said annoyed.

"And what happened then?"

"He paid and walked me to the bus. I apologised and he said things like that happen."

"So he **took it in his stride**."

Yes, he did – at least that's the way it looked from the outside. But what did he really think about me inside?

"That you're a bit more exciting than other girls!" Franzi was able to put everything back into a positive light.

But I was sure about one thing: I'd messed up the once-in-a-lifetime chance to win him over!

Later on I was lying in bed feeling frustrated and doing my best to fall asleep when my mobile phone suddenly beeped and an SMS arrived.

*I scream, you scream, everybody loves ice-cream!*

*Thanks for the* ***unforgettable*** *evening! Meik*

I stared at the display and couldn't hold back a few tears of **joy** rolling down my face.

I pressed a kiss to the sweet SMS, put the mobile phone underneath my **pillow** and **sobbed** myself happily to sleep. Perhaps a boy really could love a girl who bombarded him with ice-cream.

Not surprisingly, there was nothing more exciting for the *Pepper Dollies* the next day than to rummage around in

---

to take sth in one's stride – mit etwas gut fertig werden; unforgettable – unvergesslich; joy – Freude; pillow – Kopfkissen; to sob – schluchzen

my private life. And after they'd asked me a thousand questions in our free lesson, we **ultimately** ended up on a subject which I was really interested in: kissing. It was one of those things that everybody wanted to do, but hardly anyone did. Besides, there was kissing and kissing.

"No, but seriously, what am I meant to do if he really does want to kiss me and he won't take no for an answer?"

"What do you mean, what should you do?" Greetje was obviously surprised by the naivety of my question.

And Lea said, "I thought you really fancied him?"

"Yes, but ..." I hummed and hawed because I found the subject embarrassing even in front of my friends. "He's much older than me and ... he'll probably want to give me a **French kiss** straightaway."

There, I'd said it! I breathed a sigh of relief.

Franzi **scratched** her head thoughtfully. Obviously, the problem was clear but not cleared up.

"Well," she said in the end. "I guess you're right."

"So?"

"So what?"

"What should I do?"

"I'm afraid I can't answer that ..." Franzi grinned **shrewdly**. "You'll just have to decide for yourself."

Lea then butted in. "Well, I don't think it's such a big deal. Just wait and see. Your heart will tell you what to do."

Dear Lea's romantic soul again! She **melted** my heart!

---

ultimately – schließlich; French kiss – Zungenkuss;
to scratch – kratzen; shrewd – scharfsinnig; to melt – erweichen

But my heart was proving to be a **deceptive** thing. The things it had already said to me ... No, I was normally better off **relying** on my head. Matters of the heart weren't my thing at all anyway. In the **muddle** of feelings and stress I needed a more reliable compass than this kitschy, romantic, blood-pumping machine!

"If you **get involved with** an older boy," Franzi expanded on the subject, "then that's **part and parcel**, of course."

"It doesn't matter how old they are," Greetje added, "all boys just want to **snog** with girls. That's all they think about!"

At least the romantic Lea then gave the debate a positive turn as she said plainly and simply, "So what? If two people love each other, then each kiss is bound to be something beautiful."

Nice. But that was the big question right now: did I love Meik?

"How can I tell if I love him?"

Lea and Franzi grinned and spoke as if they were talking out of the same mouth, "If you think he tastes good!"

Hm, **tasty**!

There was a letter waiting for me at home in the post. The sender's address was marked with the logo of the City-

---

deceptive – trügerisch;
to rely – sich verlassen; muddle – Durcheinander;
to get involved with – sich einlassen mit;
part and parcel – ein wesentlicher Aspekt; to snog – knutschen;
tasty – lecker

Centre. They really had sent me a proper **contract**. A real modelling contract. I thought I was going to have a **heart attack**. I called Franzi straightaway.

"You've got to come over right now," I shouted down the phone. "You have to see this. It's got 'Modelling Contract' written in big letters at the top. A contract *between the City-Centre, as **represented** by the City-Manager, and Miss Kristina Siebert*. Did you hear that? That's me!"

"Yeah, yeah, yeah ... I'm not **deaf**. But I might go deaf if you keep screaming at me like that. Just calm down a bit, will you?"

Franzi sounded a bit annoyed. Maybe I had **worn out** with my fashion show stories over the last days (and nights). And then Meik on top.

"Oh, sorry," I said apologetically and, more importantly, a **decibel** quieter. "But we really have to celebrate this. Let's go and have a coffee together at last. Maybe Lea and Greetje want to come, too." Now that it was practically official, I could tell them about the whole thing.

But Franzi put the **brakes** on my exuberant **thirst for action** by saying she had her piano lesson in ten minutes. "Send me a fax of your contract."

That was only half the pleasure, but after she'd received it she gave me a quick call to tell me how great she thought the whole thing was.

"Just you wait, you'll end up being a real super-

---

contract – Vertrag; heart attack – Herzinfarkt;
represented – vertreten; deaf – taub;
to wear out – überstrapazieren; decibel – Dezibel;
brake – Bremse; thirst for action – Tatendrang

model!" she **smirked** and from then on the phrase 'catwalk chick' was never mentioned again.

The other girls at school, however, didn't think it was such a great idea.

The bootlicking girls, in particular, suddenly started shooting little **spiteful** arrows in my direction. It was pure envy!

They weren't actually meant to find out about it at all. I just wanted to let my closest friends in on it. But then there was an accident with the fax and, the next thing I knew, the whole school knew about it. It was so incredibly embarrassing that I was close to calling the whole thing off and **signing off sick** until the dust settled.

The evening before I had sent Franzi the first page of my contract. For some reason she then put the fax into her schoolbag and lost it at some point in school – probably when she took her sandwich out of her bag at first break.

Someone found it and, instead of giving it back to me, they decided to have a bit of fun with it: within no time it was pinned up on the school notice board in the main entrance hall. To make it worse, the **perpetrator** had drawn a big red **exclamation mark** on the fax to grab people's attention on it. Needless to say, I took the fax down straightaway when Lea told me about it, but by then almost everybody had read it and I just wanted to die.

---

to smirk – feixen; spiteful – gehässig;
to sign off sick – sich krankmelden;
perpetrator – (Übel-)Täter; exclamation mark – Ausrufezeichen

"Hey, look, here comes our supermodel!" or "Playing Claudia Schiffer, are we? What for? Do you want to catch a magician?" were two of the more harmless comments.

"Uiuiui," they aped around. "Kiki in a bikini! With a bum like hers!"

I could have **given** them all **a** good **clout**! Down, aggression, down! But it wasn't only the mademoiselles in my class who made **derisive** comments, a few of the teachers also felt the need to have their say – for purely educational reasons, of course. When even Wölfchen said I should be careful not to **neglect** school because of the fashion show and that I certainly shouldn't let the **fame** go to my head, I'd had enough.

"Dr. Wolf," I said tight-lipped. "This fashion show will make me neither famous nor rich. I just want to have some fun. It has absolutely nothing to do with school. It's just an ordinary **leisure activity**. Perhaps you'd like to **share** with us what do you do in your free-time?"

He looked puzzled at me . "I … I occasionally go fishing, but I've no idea what that's got to do with the fashion show."

"A lot," I said, still feeling livid. "Have you ever made that information public by writing it on the notice board?"

He was still unsure because he took off his glasses and started cleaning the lenses with his tie. "No, why should I?"

---

to give sb a clout – jmdm. eine schmieren; derisive – höhnisch;
to neglect – vernachlässigen; fame – Ruhm;
leisure activity – Freizeitbeschäftigung; to share – (mit-)teilen

"You see. You want your fishing hobby to remain a private matter, not to have all the **animal conservationists** accusing you of being a fish-murderer or trying to talk you out of fishing. I'm sure that would get on your nerves. And it really gets on my nerves that everybody in this school thinks they have a right to make some comment about my fashion show, just because some idiot pinned up my fax on the notice board."

I stared grimly into the class in the hope of spotting **the black sheep**, but none of my classmates outed themselves as the perpetrator. So I took a deep breath and summed up my argument with a final comment: "So, I'd be grateful if you dropped the subject now. If you still have concerns, you're more than welcome to come and see the fashion show at the beginning of May."

The *Pepper Dollies* were the first to start giggling, then some other classmates **joined in**, and soon the whole class was laughing loudly. The silence which had gripped the room during my speech was well and truly over. Nearly all of my classmates had a guilty conscience because they'd all either **slagged** me **off** or at least **teased** me meanly.

The whole time I asked myself why things like this always had to happen to me of all people and not Mona. I mean, she was also taking part in the fashion show, but no one **bad-mouthed** her for it. OK, fair enough, her con-

---

animal conservationist – Tierschützer;
the black sheep – das schwarze Schaf; to join in – einstimmen;
to slag sb off – jmdn. fertig machen; to tease – necken;
to bad-mouth sb – sich das Maul über jmdn. zerreißen

tract wasn't hanging on the notice board, but it really annoyed me that she should get out of it **unscathed**. I couldn't resist saying something. On a really **malicious** impulse I looked over to Mr Wolf again. "Why don't you show so much interest in Mona's **spiritual welfare**?" I said. "After all, she's taking part in the fashion show as well."

Wölfchen and I both looked over to Mona **simultaneously**. He must have seen how she then gave me a look that made the blood freeze in my **veins**.

Oh dear, I hadn't expected her to react as badly as that. Well, in any case the situation was now perfectly clear: I couldn't **stand** her and she almost certainly couldn't stand me. What the hell, I thought.

And when Wölfchen also started to have a go at her with his **well-meant** warnings of false hopes and irrational catwalk dreams, I enjoyed the situation with a malicious smile.

"You're horrid," said Franzi. "What you just did **isn't on**."

"I know," I said, not feeling the slightest **remorse**.

After all, it wasn't 'on' of Mona to come on to my schoolyard flirt.

---

unscathed – unbehelligt; malicious – boshaft;
spiritual welfare – Seelenheil; simultaneously – gleichzeitig;
vein – Ader; to stand sb – jmdn. leiden können;
well-meant – wohl gemeint; that's not on! – das geht nicht!;
remorse – Reue

# Tears, training, terrific guys

I was sitting over my homework in my bedroom when my guilty conscience suddenly came over me. No, what I did to Mona really wasn't on. It was unacceptable. But maybe it was her who pinned up the fax on the notice board to **get her own back** on me? I wouldn't have put it past her. Blimey, what if Meik had also read it?! That would be mega-embarrassing! Hopefully, I'd taken it down in time.

I hadn't. My mobile phone hummed its old Irish tune which I'd chosen for it. A nice tune, it was. The call was less nice though. It was Meik.

"Listen, the thing with the modelling contract is a joke, isn't it?"

So he had read it. What now? Stay cool. First hear him out. "Why?"

"**Respectable** girls don't do things like that!"

Oh no! He wasn't going to play the macho as well, was he?

"Aha?" I replied in surprise. "You know what respectable girls do then?"

---

to get one's own back – jmdm. eins auswischen;
respectable – anständig

"They don't sell their bodies, that's for sure!"

Oh you, **get a grip**! The **lad** was **out of line**.

"Do you want to discuss this right now on the mobile?" I tried to **subdue** him.

"Why not! I can hear you perfectly well!"

I wasn't talking about whether we could hear each other. I wanted to look him in the face. But if that's the way he wanted it …

"OK, so what? What do you want me to do?"

"To drop this fashion show rubbish!"

"And why? Apart from your **prejudices**, have you got an objective reason?" I was really interested in hearing what he came up with.

"It's just not you."

Oh. What a fantastic argument. I'd heard that from my dad already.

"You mean, you think I'm too ugly to do something like this?" I tried to light-heartedly make him aware of how ridiculous he was being.

But he remained **crotchety**. "I don't want to have a girlfriend who other boys **gawk** at all the time!"

Aha, now we were getting closer to the point. The guy was just plainly and simply jealous. My word, he was starting with that early. I had to **put a stop to** it straightaway. "And I don't want to have a boyfriend who guards me like a pasha guards his harem!"

---

Get a grip! – Ach du jemine!; lad – Knabe;
to be out of line – zu weit gehen; to subdue – beruhigen;
prejudice – Vorurteil; crotchety – verbiestert; to gawk – begaffen;
to put a stop to sth – einen Riegel vorschieben

He fell silent for a moment. He was speechless.

I could hear him swallow.

"You seem to have **got** completely **the wrong end of the stick** …"

Had I? I didn't think so at all.

"I just mean … Models are no more than breathing dolls. They're just there to sell something. How can you let yourself get involved with something like that?"

I started to get angry. Who did he think he was, sticking his nose into my affairs? "Well, I think it will be a lot of fun," I said, and added provocatively, "Certainly a lot more fun than your old-fashioned **moralizing sermon**."

He fell silent again for a moment. "**Shame**," he sighed. "If you change your mind, then give me a call."

"Don't hold your breath!" I snapped back at him spontaneously and hung up.

No, thank you, Dad and Wölfchen were already playing **guardians of my virtue**. I didn't need a boyfriend doing the same.

After I'd finally calmed down, I suddenly **became** painfully **aware** that maybe Meik meant what he said seriously. And that would mean … Oh no! I didn't even want to think about that!

Franzi! I had to call her straightaway.

"… and what do you think about the situation now?" I asked her after I'd told her everything.

---

to get the wrong end of the stick – etwas falsch verstehen;
moralizing sermon – Moralpredigt; Shame! – Schade!;
guardians of virtue – Tugendwächter;
to become aware – bewusst werden

"Hm, it looks like things between you two are over. If you leave him hanging like that, he can only suppose you wanted to **dump** him."

"But I didn't. I was just angry. I didn't want to dump him ..."

Franzi was silent for a moment. I could almost hear her thinking.

"If you ask me, there are only two possibilities: either you forget him or the fashion show. You can't have both."

"But I don't want to forget the fashion show!" I **howled**. "It'll be really great fun!"

"Then forget the boy!"

I woke up the next morning feeling completely **shattered**. More than one tear had trickled onto my pillow during that night as I came to realise it was over between me and Meik. Over before we'd even become a proper couple. Sniff. And today was – of all days – the first **rehearsal** for the fashion show. Just what I needed! People from the modelling agency in Berlin telling me how to walk stylishly on the catwalk! When I'd received the letter from the City-Centre a few days before, informing me that rehearsals would take place all day, I'd realised straightaway that I would never get **time off** from Wölfchen. So Mum had to deal with it.

"Mum, I need an excuse from school. For the fashion show."

---

to dump sb – jmdm. den Laufpass geben; to howl – jaulen; shattered – zerschlagen; rehearsal – Probe; time off – Beurlaubung

"No problem. I'll give you something you can take in tomorrow," she said **supportively**.

I gave a grin of relief. Mum was OK, really.

So I packed my things together. I put on my **trainers** and some comfortable clothes.

"Mum? Can I borrow a pair of **high-heeled shoes** from you? It says here that we should bring a pair with us."

I waved the letter from the agency under Mum's nose. She was still reading the newspaper at breakfast. She hadn't heard me at all. She just held up the newspaper to me and said, "Look here! That's a really nice photo of us."

With great **displeasure** I recognised the result of the campaign photo session in the market square. Hopefully, no one from my class would see it, I thought, and went straight back to my question for Mum. Fortunately, we both had the same shoe size. Mum soon found something **suitable**. Pretty high though!

I looked at the clock. I was running late as ever. I snatched up everything and hurried to the bus. I was really excited. I would soon be learning how to walk like a model, and when I strolled through the schoolyard tomorrow, Meik would be **captivated** by me, no matter what he had against models and fashion shows. The last word hadn't been spoken between us. It would be ridiculous if I couldn't win over the guy. The weapons of a woman – they were going to be **honed** today. And with a grin I thought: honed till they're razor sharp!

---

supportively – unterstützend; trainers – Turnschuhe;
high-heeled shoes – Stöckelschuhe; displeasure – Missfallen;
suitable – passend; captivated – fasziniert; to hone – wetzen

The rehearsal for the fashion show took place in a large **storeroom**. It was pretty **dreary**, badly lit and cold. The twelve girls and three boys stood around **shivering** and looking rather disoriented. I went and stood next to Debbie. Of course, Mona was there as well, with or without Wölfchen's permission, and she'd gone and stood – as you'd expect of her – right next to the boys. I took a closer look at the lads.

I'd already seen two of them at the casting, but the third boy was new, I was sure about that. You couldn't fail to notice a guy like that! I would have definitely remembered him with his dark, gelled **frizzy hair**, his thin nose, his **striking** eyebrows and … our eyes met for a second. Jeepers, he had amazing eyes! They **sparkled** with a **mischievous gleam** and the love of life! He smiled at me cheekily and presented an **impeccable** set of teeth. I lowered my head, taken aback. I expect my face was glowing red like a signalling lamp. At the same time I couldn't help thinking maybe it wasn't such a bad thing to be separated from Meik right now. I could check out the other boys without making a big deal of it. *Without making a big deal?* My inner **chaperone** sounded sceptical. *Are you aware that your internal organs are all over the place? … A **fluttering** heart … A **rumbling***

---

storeroom – Lagerraum; dreary – trist;
to shiver – frösteln; frizzy hair – Wuschelhaar;
striking – markant; to sparkle – funkeln;
mischievous gleam – Schalk; impeccable – makellos;
chaperone – Anstandsdame; to flutter – flattern;
to rumble – grummeln

*stomach ... Uneven breathing ... tzzz! Doesn't sound like it's no big deal!*

Now don't start getting sarcastic with me, I started to feel annoyed with myself and was happy when someone clapped their hands and called for my attention.

"Can someone turn on the heating, please?" asked big Verena – the girl with teeth like a horse – in the **ensuing** silence.

"No, we can't," said a young woman with **velvety** brown skin. "We haven't got any heating here. But you'll all soon warm up when we start with the choreography."

She turned to a boy who was wearing a T-shirt with the words *Berger Agency – the top in fashion* on it. He was busy fiddling around with a flashy stereo with huge **amplifiers**.

"Put on a hot number to help warm up the girls, Ali."

He **mumbled** something like "sure thing" with a strong Berlin accent and within no time Uncle Kracker was **blaring** out of the loudspeakers.

The woman with the velvety brown skin grabbed a microphone. "So, girls, I'd like to welcome you on behalf of Mrs Berger and the Centre Management. My name's Shalima, and I've been working for the Berger Agency for five years. I've worked as a model myself for ten years, so I've got a bit of experience in the business. I want to fly back to Berlin this evening, so do me a favour and **make** a bit of **an effort** today."

---

ensuing – folgend; velvety – samtig; amplifier – Verstärker;
to mumble – murmeln; to blare – dröhnen;
to make an effort – sich Mühe geben

She gave us a big smile, revealing her well-proportioned, perfectly white teeth. I couldn't help thinking of my slightly **crooked canine tooth** and decided to make a bit more effort with wearing my **brace**. Perhaps Brekkies would have been better. Damned **vanity**! On the other hand, I could never have applied to this fashion show with my mouth full of metal.

"Unfortunately, very few boys applied to be models this year – which is nothing new – so that's why we invited Percy to give Ivo and Jost some support. Percy's studying dance and has done a bit of modelling on the side. He was able to join our show at such short notice because he lives locally. Thanks a lot, Percy, it's really great you could make it!"

All the girls started to applaud enthusiastically. Percy took it coolly. He was so incredibly good-looking! I couldn't believe that a boy like him had been walking around our town and I hadn't even noticed him before! And he was almost a professional. A **shudder** of awe ran down my **spine**. It was just a bitter pill that he had to be standing next to Mona of all people. She just **gazed** at him **adoringly** the whole time.

Shalima pointed to Ali. "Ali will be doing the music throughout the show. And that ..." she pointed to a **lanky** young man in a white overall with the agency's name on it, "... that's Ken, he's the **best boy**. His main

---

crooked – schief; canine tooth – Eckzahn; brace – Zahnspange; vanity – Eitelkeit; shudder – Schauer; spine – Rückgrat; to gaze adoringly at sb – jmdn. anhimmeln; lanky – schlaksig; best boy – Mädchen für alles

areas are **decor**, the **dressing room** and photos." She clapped her hands together again and looked at Verena and a few of the elder girls. "Could you please stop chatting there?! It's going to be hard work for you all here today. If you're not up to it, then you can go now. If you don't get what this is about today, you're in the wrong place. In plain English: only the people who do exactly as I tell them will be in the show. Only they will be able to **earn** the points you need to be a winner."

"**She's off her head**," I whispered to Debbie. "She thinks she's in the **barrack square**!"

But Debbie put her finger up to her lips and murmured, "Wait and see."

All of us, including that awful Mona girl, literally **hung on** Shalima's **every word**. "First we're going to practice getting into rhythm together. Watch me while I demonstrate: four steps forward, turn, four steps back. OK?"

Shalima strode forward on her incredibly thin legs in their skin-tight leggings, did a turn in with playful **gracefulness** and came back with an arrogant smile on her face. I grinned at Debbie. Taking a few steps to some music wasn't going to be a problem for me.

Ali put on a new song and Shalima counted us in. "On four … and … one … two … three … four … and go …

---

decor – Ausstattung; dressing room – Ankleideraum;
to earn – verdienen; sb is off one's head – bei jmdm. piept es;
barrack square – Kasernenhof;
to hang on sb's every word – an jmds. Lippen hängen;
gracefulness – Anmut

and … one …two … three … four … and turn … and one … two … three … four … and turn … and …"

All of us set off **randomly** in motion at her command. Of course, it soon ended in chaos.

"Hey, can't you keep your feet to yourself?" I had a go at the girl behind me after she walked into my **heels**.

It sounded like the others were having the same problem as me. All I could hear was **swearing** and cries of pain.

"You're meant to *step* to the music, not run around the room!" said Shalima. "And if there's someone in front of you, then you can't just **flatten** them. Take smaller steps. Look what the person in front of you and behind you is doing. No one's going to win anything here if they're not willing to work as a team."

I **glanced across at** Mona. She was being a good girl, walking **in rank and file**, staring at Shalima with **servility**. Hm, I thought, although Shalima's **hullabaloo** was too authoritarian for me, if Mona can put up with it, then so can I.

So I tried to keep the person in front of me and behind me in sight and still keep moving to the rhythm of the music.

It wasn't all that easy. Particularly because I couldn't help looking at Percy.

"Good, good!" Shalima praised us in the end. "You

---

randomly – wahllos; heel – Hacke; to swear – (hier:) fluchen;
to flatten – niederwalzen;
to glance across at sb – zu jmdm. rüberschielen;
in rank and file – in Reih und Glied; servility – Unterwürfigkeit;
hullabaloo – Getue

seem to have got a grasp of the rhythm, but most of you move like **cattle** at feeding time."

That was encouraging.

"Your front leg always has to be slightly in front of your **pivot leg**. Like this ..." She gave a demonstration and I was amazed to see how the hips swung by themselves. Incredible. That's exactly how Mona walked over the schoolyard. What a simple trick! I gave Shalima a grateful smile and immediately tried it out myself.

Debbie giggled. "Cool."

I glanced across at Percy. He smiled in acknowledgement.

"Now you can put on your high-heels."

Oh no, I would ruin the good impression I'd made straightaway.

Shalima pointed to Mona and me. "You two come here."

Mona and I stared at each other. Mona had an arrogant look in her eye and she looked at me from head to foot. She grinned **contemptuously** and, as we stood side by side, she hissed to me, "So, borrowed Mummy's shoes, did we? They look pretty **worn-out** to me. Make sure you don't **trip up** in them!"

Grr! I looked at her feet which were, of course, in **the latest slingbacks**. Where on earth did she get the money for cool things like that?

---

cattle – Vieh; pivot leg – Standbein;
contemptuously – geringschätzig; worn-out – ausgelatscht;
to trip up – stolpern;
the latest slingbacks – die neuesten Slingpumps

"Now come on! Let's go!" said Shalima impatiently.

Ali put on a new CD. "Let's dance ... dadam ... dadadam ... Let's dance ..."

Mona set off and I wobbled along next to her in Mum's "pumps". As we went past Ivo, Jost and Percy my cheeks **flushed** with embarrassment. They became even redder when I heard Percy whistle quietly. I just hoped I wouldn't twist my **ankle**, I thought and sighed with relief as we got to Shalima.

"OK," she said. "If you two give it a bit more practice, it could work out. You two perform together."

I had no idea what she was talking about, but I did understand one thing: I was **saddled with** Mona! What did I do to deserve that?

"We're going to be presenting fashion from five different **suppliers** during each show. Each show will **consist of** ten to fifteen **sets**. Each set has its own theme. That means you'll have to get changed a few times in between sets."

Shalima's words made everyone groan out loud.

"Of course, we'll practice that together," she immediately comforted us. Then she clapped her hands and asked us to get into pairs and **swap** clothes with each other. "It's a **confidence-building** exercise," she said. "It calls for team spirit."

"Is she serious?" I asked Debbie. "I'm not getting un-

---

to flush – erröten; ankle – Knöchel;
to be saddled with – am Hals haben; supplier – Anbieter;
to consist of sth – aus etwas bestehen; set – Bild;
to swap – tauschen; confidence-building – vertrauensbildend

dressed down to my underwear here in front of the boys. There was no mention of that in the contract!"

"Then let's get changed in the toilets," she suggested.

We were just trying to quietly escape when Shalima blocked our path. "Where are you going?"

"To the toilet," I said, although I knew she could tell I was lying.

"Not in the kindergarten by any chance?"

The older girls laughed.

"Stop making such a fuss. You won't get far in this business with false **modesty**. Either you do as I say, or you can go home right now. It's your choice."

I spotted Mona looking at me. She was already in her underwear and seemed to be literally **revelling in** our **disgrace**.

Just you wait, I thought, I'll show you. Don't even think I'll leave the field open to you without a fight.

"OK, then I'll go to the toilet later," I said **nonchalantly**. "There's bound to be a break sometime."

Everybody else had already chosen a partner, so I had to exchange clothes with Debbie. Seeing as she was half a head shorter than me and was pretty **petite** to boot, the exercise had a certain comedy about it. Whereas my clothes **flapped** around Debbie's **limbs**, I had to squeeze into her tight jeans, and my stomach **bulged** over the **zip** really embarrassingly.

---

modesty – Schamhaftigkeit;
to revel in sth – sich an etwas weiden; disgrace – Blamage;
nonchalantly – lässig; petite – zierlich; to flap – schlottern;
limb – Glieder; to bulge – quellen; zip – Reißverschluss

After Mona maliciously commented in passing, "A bit of a diet wouldn't do you any harm," I could only comfort myself with the sight of the 1,90-m-tall Verena: her partner's skirt was hanging around her hips like a **loincloth**.

I couldn't help glancing across at Percy again. He really had a great body. And that brown skin of his! He looked like he'd just come back from two weeks in Mallorca – which really was where his **suntan** came from as I found out later! He'd brought it home with him from a "fantastic photo session".

The exercise did **achieve** one thing, however: everybody was a lot less **tense** afterwards. We all laughed a lot – which felt really good – and after that the mood was really easy-going. People **kidded around**, made jokes about each other and said a lot of encouraging things. I guessed this was exactly what Shalima had wanted to achieve with her exercise. Unfortunately, Shalima put Debbie into another group, with girls the same size as her. As she'd already said, I had to go into a group with Mona. Didn't someone say I'd really enjoy this fashion show?

But when the DJ put on Jennifer Lopez's hit, *Love don't cost a thing*, and I caught Percy looking at me admiringly, I let myself **get swept away**. Oh, how **sublime** it would be, striding out onto the catwalk in a really chic outfit to this music.

---

loincloth – Lendenschurz; suntan – Sonnenbräune;
to achieve – erreichen; tense – angespannt;
to kid around – herumalbern;
to get swept away – sich mitreißen lassen; sublime – erhaben

During lunch break we went to pick up our shoes from the shoe boutique. After that I joined Debbie again. All the models were allowed to order food and a drink in the Centre restaurant. Debbie and I helped ourselves to a healthy portion at the salad buffet and ordered **turkey breast**. As Mona walked past our table balancing her tray, I had the **fleeting** impression she wanted to join us. But my icy look warned her off just in time. No, I couldn't be doing with her right now. Not now when I had an opportunity to have a **gossip** with Debbie about the others.

"What do you think of them all?" I asked Debbie **bluntly**, having just sat down at the table.

"Really sweet! All three of them! A great mixture," she answered promptly and gave a silly giggle.

"And Percy? What do you think of him?"

Debbie giggled again. "Beautiful!" she said **ardently**.

"Beautiful?" What kind of thing was that to say about a boy? "Boys aren't beautiful," I said.

"Yes they are," insisted Debbie **unreasonably**. "Percy is beautiful. Like a Greek god! Did you see his body? Really muscular but thin ... when he walks, he looks **wiry**, but his skin is still smooth ... And those **eyelashes** ... it's almost a crime that Mother Nature wastes eyelashes like his on a boy."

I looked at Debbie sceptically. Crikey, that was an almost lyrical outburst! Had she fallen for him?

---

turkey breast – Putenschnitzel; fleeting – flüchtig;
gossip – Schwätzchen; bluntly – unverblümt;
ardently – inbrünstig; unreasonable – uneinsichtig;
wiry – drahtig; eyelashes – Wimpern

"No, no," she denied my indiscreet **enquiry**. "Not at all. I'm being purely objective. But he's the best-looking boy I've ever seen **in the flesh**. He reminds me of that actor from *Ice-cream Soda*."

"*Ice-cream Soda*? Are you sure that's the title of a film?"

I couldn't remember it at all. The last film I saw with a lot of ice was *Titanic* and ... whatever ... I decided to **keep an eye on** this Percy.

"How old do you think he is?"

"Eighteen or nineteen, maybe even twenty. He's far too old for us. Unfortunately." Debbie gave a frustrated sigh.

I sighed as well and immediately followed it up with a scream: "I don't believe it!" I cried and nodded to the table where Mona was sitting with two other models.

What I saw there made me turn red with anger.

In front of Mona's table stood none other than Percy. And he was just about to sit down. I wanted to run over to him and **beg** him to come over to our table, but what possible reason could I have given him to do that? Mona had **the plague** or **chickenpox**? Mona stinks of **garlic**? She's a witch – if you sit at her table, she'll turn you into her slave? I feared the latter was closest to the truth, but it wasn't exactly a convincing argument. But what a pain. What did that silly cow have that I didn't?

---

enquiry – Nachfrage; in the flesh – leibhaftig;
to keep an eye on sb – jmdn. im Auge behalten;
to beg – anflehen; the plague – die Pest;
chickenpox – Windpocken; garlic – Knoblauch

"Why? Why are all the boys crazy about Mona?"

We were on the way back to the training hall after lunch, and Debbie had to put up with all my frustration again.

"For crying out loud, girl, have you got an **inferiority complex** or something?" she asked irritably.

Hm, I heard that one often enough from Franzi. Maybe there was an element of truth in it? I decided to try and work on myself a bit. Debbie thought that was a good idea.

"Smile!" she said encouragingly. "And keep smiling!"

We spent the afternoon in rehearsals and this time the boys joined in.

All of a sudden, without any warning, Shalima picked Mona out of our group and said, "You perform with the boys!"

Envy isn't the right word to describe what I felt at that moment. Why did Mona have to have such luck again? I expect she wrapped Percy around her little finger at lunch. I looked away **in disgust**. But then someone grabbed me by the arm and I **spun around**.

"You ... what's your name?" asked Shalima.

"Krist ... Krist ... Kiki!" I stuttered.

"You perform with the boys as well. The five of you can do the last set before the finale."

She dragged me away from Debbie to the middle of the hall where Mona was already giggling with the boys.

"Ali, put on *Follow me*, and you guys can go onto your

---

inferiority complex – Minderwertigkeitskomplex;
in disgust – angewidert; to spin around – herumfahren

positions ... Ivo here, Mona, Percy, Kiki, Jost here. Percy starts: dance solo, please!"

Percy stepped forward and did a quick break-dance solo. Then he stayed at the front, and Ivo and Jost joined him **crosswise**.

"Now you two, Mona, Kiki." Shalima nodded at us.

Mona immediately started moving. I completely messed up my **cue** and didn't move an inch. And again! This time I **tore off** and Mona was left standing.

Shalima was annoyed. "Couldn't you try and do it together? We want to finish today."

The third time around it worked out OK. Crikey, it was exciting! I was actually meant to do a set with Percy, with the greatest guy who had ever made a catwalk unsafe! It was just a shame that Mona had to be there. But nothing's perfect in life. I probably looked quite **sullen** at the thought because Shalima shouted, "Come on, don't forget to smile!" at me.

Did I really have to? If only I could just press a button and smile. Was I a **nuclear power station** or what? How can you **dispel** frustration and bring in the sunshine?

Apart from Mona and the boys, I was also doing a set with May, a black British girl, and with some girl called Cindy who thought that she was above everybody else because she'd already won Face of the Month in some youth magazine. *"The most boring face in town"* would have been more suitable! And – inevitably enough – I

---

crosswise – über Kreuz; cue – Einsatz; to tear off – lospreschen; sullen – missmutig; nuclear power station – Atomkraftwerk; to dispel – vertreiben

was also saddled with Mona in that group. What a pain! Shalima then told us about the **running order** for the fashion show and gave us a few tips.

"So, girls," she said, "I expect you to **shave** your **armpits** and not to walk around here with legs like a monkey. You might have to present **sleeveless** tops and short skirts and shorts."

Oh my giddy aunt, I thought, I'd never shaved myself before. How was I meant to do that – borrow Dad's razor?

"Your mum's bound to have a lady shaver," Debbie answered my question with a whisper.

Did she?

"And you should all come in **skin-coloured** underwear. You might have to wear items that are very light or **transparent**."

Everybody started giggling, and I just thought I was completely **out of place** here. Me in a see-through top! I'd rather jump from the catwalk!

"You should all wear **tights**, but only **seamless** ones and no **reinforced** toes and heels. Your make-up will be done by a stylist from the perfume shop, so don't put on more than some **foundation**. Please make sure your hair's freshly washed. Your hair will be done by someone from Klimmt Hairdresser's."

---

running order – Ablauf; to shave – rasieren;
armpit – Achselhöhle; sleeveless – ärmellos;
skin-coloured – hautfarben; transparent – durchsichtig;
out of place – fehl am Platz; tights – Strumpfhosen;
seamless – nahtlos; reinforced – verstärkt;
foundation – Grundierung

We were all a bit groggy at the end of the day, but Shalima was pleased, and that was all that mattered. And for me only one thing counted as well: Percy's smile. When he called over to me before going and said "Ciao, bella" in a really **laid-back** way, I felt like a hundred violins were playing just for me – no, rubbish, not violins, drums – big, banging drums! *Do you feel my heart beating ... or ... am I only dreaming?*

By the time I called each of the *Pepper Dollies* in the evening, I had quite a lot to tell. I was so **exhausted**, I had to keep it short. I promised them more in our free lesson the next day in school. But there was one thing that I wanted to know from Franzi before I hung up: "Do you shave your armpits?"

She giggled. "No, but I did think about it once. I get hair there like a **jungle**. Why do you ask?"

I told her what Shalima had said.

"Oh, good," she answered, "then you can try it out and tell me what it's like."

Well, great! I just loved being a **guinea pig**.

"Mum?" I asked after dinner as the Joker threw himself in front of the **box** to watch the charts on some music channel, "have you got a few minutes for a girls' talk?"

She got that **mother-hen** look on her face, which usu-

---

laid-back – locker, lässig; exhausted – erschöpft; jungle – Urwald; guinea pig – Meerschweinchen, (hier:) Versuchskaninchen; box – (ugs.) Glotze; mother-hen – Glucke

ally made me turn around and run, but this time I had no other choice than to put up with it.

"Of course, of course," she answered, "if I can be of any help ..."

"You can." I immediately took her up on her offer of help. "I need some tights, foundation make-up and ..." – dramatic pause – "skin-coloured underwear." And so she didn't think you-know-what, I quickly added by way of an explanation, "It's all for the fashion show."

The speculative curiosity, which had just darted across her face, immediately disappeared.

"No problem," she said. "I can help you out there. But I suggest you go and buy the underwear yourself with Franzi. The City-Centre contract can cover that."

I smiled at her **gratefully**. That was easier than I'd expected. I was just about to head off to bed when I turned around and asked, "Uhm, Mum, have you got a lady shaver?"

Mum must have **picked up** that I found the question embarrassing because she laughed and said, "Why? Do you want to borrow that as well?"

"Er, well, uhm ..." I hummed and hawed. "Shalima said ... well ... for my legs and armpits ..."

Mum started to giggle like a really silly schoolgirl. "Right, right ... got it! It's in the bathroom. You go ahead. I'll be right there to show you how it works."

What was so funny? I went upstairs to my parents' bathroom **in** a bit of **a huff**.

---

gratefully – dankbar; to pick up – (hier:) bemerken;
in a huff – eingeschnappt

When, shortly afterwards, Mum handed me the cold, **well-designed** shaver, I was glad she was there to help me. I didn't want to shave my skin off instead of my hair.

The next day I had a really bad **headache**. I looked out of the window to see if there'd been a change in the weather, but the only thing that had changed was clearly inside of me. I'd gone crazy. I'd spent the whole night dreaming about boys. And not just any boys, not fantastic princes in shining armour in faraway lands. No. About real, **tangible** guys – so real I could almost touch them!

That had never happened to me before. And the strangest thing of all was that I'd dreamed about Meik and Percy both at the same time.

If that wasn't **suspect**! Had I fallen in love with both of these mysterious **creatures** at the same time?

I went into the bathroom to get my cool head back under the shower.

Wölfchen was, of course, anything other than **thrilled** when I gave him my excuse. Mona was also on the receiving end of his displeasure.

"I can't stop your parents from letting you participate in such events but, even with the best will in the world, I can't accept the fashion show as a proper excuse not to come to lessons. This will go on your reports as a day of **absence**."

---

well-designed – formschön; headache – Kopfschmerzen; tangible – greifbar; suspect – verdächtig; creature – Wesen; thrilled – begeistert; absence – Abwesenheit

He curtly put away the letters of excuse and wrote something in the class book with a **frown** on his face. Later on, in the break, we read what he had written. He really had meant what he said: *Mona and Kristina were absent without an excuse.*

What a killjoy!

In the main break I saw Meik standing alone at the drinks dispenser. I was just **dying to** try out my newly **acquired** modelling tricks and win him back.

"Wait here a moment," I said to the *Pepper Dollies.* "There's something I have to do."

I stood up straight just as he happened to look over to me. I raised my right hand and waved tentatively.

He smiled, but otherwise didn't move an inch.

So, that left me with no other choice than to go over to him – while he was looking at me. The ideal opportunity to try out my new, stylish way of walking. What if he thought I had a problem in my hips again? The thought made me feel sick. Oh, rubbish! After all, I'd spent a whole day practising it. I'd just have to imagine that some music was playing. Three … four … *come along now … come along with me* … I held my head up high and strode over to him, carefully placing one foot in front of the other, my toothpaste smile on my face.

Someone did actually wolf-whistle at me. Well, it wasn't one wolf whistle actually, it was an entire concert of wolf whistles, and they didn't come from Meik, as

---

frown – Stirnrunzeln;
to be dying to do sth – darauf brennen, etwas zu tun;
to acquire – erwerben

I'd hoped. They came from behind me. I turned around and saw Fabian and a load of guys from my class.

"Very professional!" said Fabian **approvingly**. I even got the impression he meant it seriously. But because this was all happening in front of Meik, I found it really embarrassing. What on earth would he think?

When I turned back to him, I saw him coming up to me.

"Eh, Meik, eh, I ... there's something I have to tell you ..." I started to stutter, but he didn't want to hear. He just grabbed my hand and pulled me away.

"Let's get away from these unqualified lads," he said.

Shortly afterwards we were sitting on a **secluded** bench near the sports field. Meik was sticking **stubbornly** to his prejudices.

"You see what happens if you make a display of yourself?!" he said, and I thought my dad was sitting next to me.

That was **a real turn-off**!

"I'm not making a display of myself. I'm presenting fashion!" I said somewhat louder that I intended. "I'm not responsible for boys being **horny**!"

He **winced** a bit at the **ferocity** of my reaction, but – because he obviously had the feeling that he'd gone too far himself – he said apologetically, "I just think the whole fashion business is completely **superfluous**."

---

approving – beifällig; secluded – abgelegen;
stubbornly – dickköpfig; to be a real turn-off – abtörnen;
horny – geil; to wince – zusammenzucken;
ferocity – Heftigkeit; superfluous – überflüssig

He had such an honest look in those blue eyes of his as he said this, that I couldn't do anything but forgive him.

"Oh, you know, **it just came up**," I said. "My mum is doing the advertising for the fashion show. It's an interesting experience and after all ..." I just couldn't help saying it: "... Mona's doing it as well."

"Mona? The brunette from the bus. She's really good-looking as well."

I looked at him in amazement. That was an interesting comment. So he thought she was good-looking! Well, well! And it didn't seem to **bother** him at all that *she* was taking part in the fashion show. To hell with Mona!

"You can come to the fashion show if you want," I said brusquely, trying to get Mona out of my head. "Then you can see for yourself that there are no **peeping Toms** trying to look up my skirt." Oh, for crying out loud, what did I say that for? Talk about the wrong tone.

But Meik managed to ignore this **harsh rebuke**. "I like a girl who's got a mind of her own," he said with a laugh. "But I still think this fashion show rubbish is stupid. Still, if you think it's fun ... The main thing is you stand by your own actions."

Now he was making me really curious. "And you? Do you stand by your actions?"

He was just about to answer when the school bell rang for the end of break. What a shame. His answer would have interested me.

---

it just came up – es hat sich so ergeben; to bother – stören;
peeping Tom – Spanner; harsh – schroff;
rebuke – Zurechtweisung

Meik didn't seem to be particularly thrilled about the sudden **interruption** either. "Would you mind if we continued this conversation after school?" he asked hesitantly.

I shook my head. "Sure we can. It's my last free afternoon. The fashion show week starts tomorrow."

"Where shall we meet?"

Yes, where then? Preferably in some romantic place!!! "We could go for a walk ..."

He nodded.

"At the **gravel pit**?"

He nodded. And so we agreed to meet there at 6 o'clock in the evening.

---

interruption – Unterbrechung; gravel pit – Kiesgrube

# Catwalk cows

I took Sniffy with me as a **chaperone**. She was over the moon and, after she'd given Meik a good sniffing at, she gave him the OK. He had a really natural way with her, and I could tell that he liked animals. A bonus for him.

We took a walk around the former gravel pit, which had been filled with water, and had a lively discussion about everything under the sun.

The only thing we didn't talk about was the fashion show. It was still a **touchy subject** between us. As **dusk** began to fall, we sat down on the **embankment** with Sniffy between us and watched the sun go down. The sun was just turning into a circle of orange and red when Meik suddenly picked up Sniffy and put her down on his **lap**. At the same time he **slipped** a bit **closer** to me. He started to stroke Sniffy with one hand and me with the other – the dog strongly, me **timidly**. I let him touch me and he **plucked up his courage** and started to stroke my hair a bit as well. The sun began to sink slowly behind the

---

chaperone – Anstandsdame; touchy subject – heikles Thema;
dusk – Dämmerung; embankment – Böschung; lap – Schoß;
to slip closer – näher rücken; timidly – zaghaft;
to pluck up one's courage – seinen Mut zusammennehmen

town's skyline. Then Meik stopped stroking me and put his arm around me **tightly**. I gave a shiver and he pulled me towards his shoulder where I felt in good hands. I lay in his arms for a long time.

*Do you feel my heart beating ... or am I only dreaming ... do you feel the same ... I don't wanna lose this feeling ... is this burning an eternal flame?*

The fashion show music – it was just perfect for this wonderful moment. But it was anything but perfect when I suddenly saw Percy's **handsome** face in front of me as Meik leaned towards me to kiss me! I turned away embarrassed. I couldn't do that to him – kiss him while thinking about another boy!

The sun finally set. Then we got to our feet and went our separate ways at the bus – unkissed. What a really tragic situation.

When I got home with Sniffy, I rushed straight to the phone to call Franzi, but she wasn't at home. What an **intolerable** situation! Who could I talk to about this **memorable** date? Not the Joker?

"I understand a lot about love," he said as I went into the kitchen and started making myself a cup of tea in frustration. "I know you had a date with Meik, and I bet you didn't kiss him!"

**I beg your pardon**? Had my brother mutated into the oracle of love?

---

tightly – fest; handsome – gut aussehend;
intolerable – unerträglich; memorable – denkwürdig;
I beg your pardon? – Wie bitte?

"What makes you think that?" I asked him curiously.

"You don't look too happy."

He really was a little psychologist!

"People who have kissed **float** three centimetres above the floor."

Oh really?

"Or they knock everything over because they see the world through a pink **wad of cotton wool**."

Oh, right!

"On top of that, they keep singing or **humming** to themselves."

Hm.

"You're not doing any of those things. Which means you haven't kissed."

"Congratulations!" I said. "An absolutely brilliant **deduction** – but, unfortunately, it's wrong! He *did* kiss me!" And with this lie I left my completely flabbergasted little brother standing in the kitchen. After I'd drunk the first cup of tea in my bedroom, I was **overwhelmed** by remorse and I had a guilty conscience to boot. What if I'd destroyed the Joker's belief in the truth of **scientifically proven findings**? Might I have just ruined his possible future career as a **researcher**? No, I couldn't take the **blame** for that. I opened my bedroom door. "Hey, Joker!" I called out into the corridor. "Come here!"

---

to float – schweben; wad of cotton wool – Wattebausch;
to hum – summen; deduction – Schlussfolgerung;
to overwhelm – überwältigen;
scientifically proven findings – wissenschaftliche Beweisführungen; researcher – Forscher; blame – Schuld

He strolled past with a seriously cool expression on his face.

"You're right. We didn't kiss. He wanted to, but I didn't."

"No? Why not? Meik's a nice guy. I bet he's going to be **head boy**!"

"Well, in that case!" I sighed. "I don't know either. But maybe it will happen someday."

He **patted** my hand encouragingly. "It'll work out," he said **precociously**. "All girls are scared of the first time."

If I hadn't been so tactful, I would have burst out laughing. To hear something like that from the mouth of a Year 5 boy!

"That's a very dramatic **development**," said Lea the next morning at school. "Kiki's going to have to decide who she's going to give her love to."

Oh, no, it was far too early to talk about love. Sure, both boys seemed to be really nice at first sight, but what else did I know about them? Certainly not enough to even mention the word love. Lea was a little bit too romantic. These days a woman didn't just fall for the first man she came across. She had to test him out first to see if he **kept** his **promises**. Franzi took the role of realist again in our group.

"Well, I don't see any problem at all. It's better to have

---

head boy – Schulsprecher; to pat – tätscheln;
precociously – altklug;
development – Entwicklung;
to keep a promise – ein Versprechen halten

a choice between two guys rather than none. Kiki will choose the right one when the time is **ripe**."

Thanks for the **vote of confidence**, I thought, although I wasn't at all sure if it was **justified**.

In the main break I looked furtively over to the corner of the schoolyard where Meik and his mates were standing around. I wondered if he was angry because the evening didn't go the way he'd planned? All of a sudden, he looked over to me – as if he'd sensed my eyes upon him – and laughed really sweetly. Then he turned back to his friends.

Well, he certainly didn't seem to be angry.

In the next lesson I was anything but **attentive**. My **impending** catwalk premiere was making me nervous. Unfortunately, my teachers had little sympathy with me, and I was on the receiving end of more than one warning. When the bell finally rang at the end of the day, I saw to it that I got home as quickly as possible. I had to take a shower and wash my hair. Fortunately, Mum was at home, and she helped me put on my foundation. That was a **stroke of luck**! After all, I don't normally wear make-up! She did it with a few **skilful** movements of the hand. After my hair had dried, I threw on a few comfy clothes, packed all the things I needed together and **dashed off**.

---

ripe – reif; vote of confidence – Vertrauensbeweis;
to justify – etwas rechtfertigen; attentive – aufmerksam;
impending – bevorstehend; a stroke of luck – ein Glücksfall;
skilful – geschickt; to dash off – losdüsen

"And don't forget to come around!" I called before I shut the front door.

When I got to the City-Centre, I was really **bowled over**. They'd built a T-shaped catwalk in the middle of the open foyer and divided up the backstage with **partitions** for the quick changes between sets. Everything was very stylish, and the **advertising boards** from Mum's agency looked really **high-grade**. The music system had been set up backstage, too, and there were huge amplifiers either side of the catwalk. There were loads of **lush** plants artistically arranged in the corners and niches. But I wasn't the only one who immediately got **stage fright** at the sight of this professional setting. My nerves began to jangle.

"I bet I fall off the catwalk," said Debbie. "I've got a sneaking suspicion that something's going to go really wrong."

"Oh, that's just stage fright. Don't get all worked up over nothing," I tried to comfort her half-heartedly.

"Where shall we get changed?" I asked Shalima, who was **bustling around** busily.

She pointed to a door to the **stairwell**.

When I opened the door, I was gobsmacked.

The stairwell didn't lead to the dressing room, it *was* the dressing room. The other models were **milling around** in the narrow spaces between **clothes rails** on

---

bowled over – überwältigt; partition – Trennwand;
advertising board – Werbetafel; high-grade – edel; lush – üppig;
stage fright – Lampenfieber; to bustle around – herumwuseln;
stairwell – Treppenhaus; to mill around – umherlaufen;
clothes rail – Kleiderständer

wheels and a few chairs. Some of them were already in their skin-coloured underwear, ready to slip on the fashion items they were going to present. Others were drinking coffee out of paper cups and chatting, or were more or less calmly watching the others rushing around.

The only three male models were standing in the middle of all this **commotion** with a grin on their faces. As I spotted Percy, **my heart missed a beat**. Then it beat twice as fast. What a great guy! All ready for the show, he looked even better today than during rehearsals. He immediately gave me a friendly smile while Ivo gave his entire attention to Verena, who was flirting openly with him. Well, if he was into horse faces ... Jost had just taken off his sweatshirt and was standing topless in front of a clothes rail. Percy was also in the middle of changing. While I was watching, he **unzipped** his jeans. I had to take a deep breath, but then I turned away.

"We're not all meant to get changed here together, are we?" I said to Debbie because I just couldn't believe what I was seeing.

"I'm afraid so," she said, also slightly shocked. "That's why we had to do that clothes-swapping exercise during rehearsals!" And she put on a voice to imitate Shalima: "No false modesty, girls!"

We were still rooted to the spot in front of the open door as a few girls called, "Close the door! There's a **draught**!" and I felt someone push me gently in the back.

---

commotion – Trubel;
my heart missed a beat – mir stockte das Herz;
to unzip – Reißverschluss aufmachen; draught – Luftzug

Mrs Berger, the boss of the modelling agency in person, escorted me into the stairwell with a slight **shove**. "Come on, in you go, girls! What's the matter? Get a move on! The show's about to begin."

She noticed that we hesitated.

"Is there a problem?" she asked.

"Uhm, yes, the boys ... er ..."

"Oh, for goodness sake!" she laughed. "They don't **bite**!"

But I wasn't the only one who found the situation a bit uncomfortable. Mrs Berger, however, just said that a stairwell wasn't exactly the ideal changing room, but a very **common** one at events like this.

I guess it was also perfectly normal for members of the audience not to read the sign saying "**No entry** – Fashion show!", ignore the **cordon** and come into our "changing room". The fact that we were all freezing our backsides off in there and getting a cold was a **side effect** which she hadn't reckoned with either.

Mrs Berger clapped her hands together and addressed the gathered team.

"So, girls," she said. "This may be a competition, but I hope everything remains on a fair and friendly basis. Shalima will keep a points list every day and remember: what counts isn't just how you perform, but how you handle your clothes and, above all, how **considerate** you are to each other. No one can afford to get bitchy, right?

---

shove – Schubs; to bite – beißen; common – üblich;
no entry – Zutritt verboten; cordon – Absperrung;
side effect – Nebeneffekt; considerate – kollegial

OK, give your best for a good show. And – as we say in the business – break a leg!"

She swept off after finishing her speech, leaving behind the scent of **lilies of the valley** and lavender.

Shalima, who had turned up in the **meantime**, took a closer look at me and Debbie. "You two haven't done your hair or put on your make-up. Come on, off with you to the hairdresser. You have to do that before getting dressed. **Chop, chop**!" And she **shooed** us out of the room like a couple of chicks in a **chicken run**.

"Where is the hairdresser's?" asked Debbie.

I seemed to remember having seen it on the first floor, and so we took the panoramic lift up. The catwalk looked fantastic from up there!

There were a few other models "**in progress**" at the hairdresser's. An unfriendly woman pushed me over to a chair and said, "Take a seat here. It'll be your turn in a minute."

I sat down – only to jump up a fraction of a second later because sitting next to me was none other than … Mona! She looked pretty unhappy, so I sat back down again to enjoy the sight. It was with a certain pleasure that I watched her hair being messed up by a **bad-tempered** hairdresser. Smile! I waited for what felt like an **eternity** until a make-up artist finally came over to me. She circled my eyes with eyeliner, dabbed eye shadow on my

---

lily of the valley – Maiglöckchen; meantime – Zwischenzeit;
Chop, chop! – Hopp, hopp!; to shoo – scheuchen;
chicken run – Hühnerhof; in progress – zugange;
bad-tempered – schlecht gelaunt; eternity – Ewigkeit

eyelids, and put thick mascara onto my eyelashes, which really did make them look considerably longer.

"What are you going to be wearing?" she asked when it came to the question of choosing a suitable colour for my lipstick. I had no idea what outfit I'd be presenting, so she chose a discreet red. "That **matches** most things. Just let me know if you want to have a different colour tomorrow." Then she quickly dabbed a bit of rouge onto my cheeks and there I was: ready to go!

Great! Just to have taken part in this make-up session made the fashion show **worth it** already.

The situation in the chair next to me had **escalated** dramatically in the meantime. Mona's **piled-up hairdo** had **collapsed** for the second time. She was really angry and was having a go at the hairdresser for being so incompetent. All the hairdresser could do was **sob**. "There's nothing I can do about it!" she moaned. "What am I supposed to do if there aren't any more **hairpins** and clips? Nobody told us we were going to have to do the hair for all these models today."

I couldn't help **gloating** with anything but a sense of team spirit.

I was very happy with my hairdresser. She was called Desiree and she wasn't only sweet, she was a master of her **craft**. She'd conjured up an extravagant piled-up hair-

---

to match – passen; it's worth it – es lohnt sich;
to escalate – sich zuspitzen; piled-up hairdo – Hochfrisur;
to collapse – zusammenbrechen; to sob – schluchzen;
hairpin – Haarnadel; to gloat – mit Schadenfreude betrachten;
craft – Handwerk

do in no time at all. I never found out where she got the extra hairpins from.

"Hang onto them and bring them with you tomorrow," she said to me as I thanked her **effusively**.

"You look fantastic!" said Debbie, and I could only give the compliment back. Both of us looked like we'd just stepped out of a **glossy magazine**. As we went back to the changing room, Mona was still arguing with her hairdresser and fighting to save her hairdo.

"Do you think the two of them will sort it out today?" I giggled and secretly hoped that they wouldn't because at least I would be rid of her then.

In the meantime, the mood in the stairwell had grown somewhat tense. A couple of girls had succeeded in making each other nervous. They didn't like the clothes they were wearing, so they kept going up to each other to seek **reassurances**. They just wanted to hear that they looked absolutely fabulous. It went like this: "Don't I look awful? Go on, tell me I look awful … like a walking sack of potatoes! Go on, feel free. You can say it. Be honest. Don't I look awful? Like a walking sack of potatoes …"

Another girl had **got into a state** about her lipstick being the wrong colour. "Terrible! How can you have red lipstick with a purple pullover?!"

And another girl was complaining about her shoes. "I'm getting **blisters** already! I'll never make it!"

Shalima took all of this in her stride and remained sur-

---

effusively – überschwänglich;
glossy magazine – Hochglanzmagazin; reassurance – Bestätigung; to get into a state – durchdrehen; blister – Blase

prisingly calm. She comforted each and every one of them. "Your clothes really suit you," she would say. "Only you could wear that!" Or: "Red is in this season – especially with purple. Bright is beautiful!" Or: "You should have chosen a pair of shoes that fitted you. Change them after the show today. And no false modesty! Take a size larger!"

But when May wanted to swap her T-shirt for mine because she thought it suited her outfit better, Shalima's patience reached its limit.

"What a **daft bat**!" she said just as the City-Manager came through the door to drive us all mad with a completely **trivial** speech.

All the boutiques had received a photograph of each model with their **vital statistics**. The boutiques made their selection on the basis of these photos. They then put together small collections for the individual groups. Ken and a handful of salesgirls had brought all the clothes down to us on mobile clothes rails. After the show everything had to be brought back and neatly hung up.

"You're the classic sporty type," Shalima had immediately put me into a category, and so I was hardly surprised to find out what I would be wearing for the first set. Everybody in the set would be in black and white, and I was meant to wear a smart black **trouser suit** with a white blouse. I looked for a place to get changed behind one of the clothes rails, out of sight of curious **onlookers**.

---

daft bat – Zimperzicke; trivial – belanglos;
vital statistics – Körpermaße; trouser suit – Hosenanzug;
onlooker – Schaulustige

"Tomorrow I'll bring a **sheet** with me," I said to Debbie. "We can use it as a **screen**." She thought that was a really good idea.

This made Mrs Berger smile slightly, but Shalima said dryly, "You don't happen to be a bit **inhibited** by any chance, sweetheart? If you want to become a model, you'll have to **get over** that."

Become a model? Me?! "Do you actually think I could become a model?"

"Of course, why not?" she said laughing at my timid question. "But like I said, you've got a lot to learn!"

Well, that's what I was here for.

As I was getting changed into my smart trouser suit behind the clothes rails, Percy whistled through his teeth. "Oh la la, bella!" he said and his smile was pure enthusiasm.

He certainly had an **expressive** face! He should become an actor, I thought.

When I caught sight of myself in the mirror, I froze in awe. I didn't just look a lot older, I looked absolutely **divine**. It was as if a good **fairy** had just waved her **wand** over little **Cinderella** and transformed her into a princess.

Don't try and tell me that clothes don't make people. My mistrust of the make-the-most-of-yourself articles in women's and fashion magazines suddenly disap-

---

sheet – Laken; screen – Trennwand;
inhibited – verklemmt;
to get over sth – über etwas hinwegkommen;
expressive – ausdrucksstark; divine – überirdisch;
fairy – Fee; wand – Zauberstab; Cinderella – Aschenputtel

peared. With a bit of styling and colour it really was possible. I tried to imagine what I could do with a few of the bootlickers, but the idea of transforming them into beauties was too much even for my imagination. They just didn't have any **flair**.

And, thinking of the bootlickers, I couldn't help thinking of Mona again. Where had she got to? Had she lost the fight with the hairdresser? I really wouldn't mind if she missed the show, I thought. But I **relished** the idea too soon. Just then Mona came into the stairwell, freshly made up and her hair done. There were only a few tiny **braids** on the side of her hair left over from the piled-up hairdo. After all that fuss!

She looked pretty livid. Shalima, however, didn't notice this. "**Look lively**, girl!" she said. "And make sure you're punctual next time, please!"

That was too much for Mona after the torture she'd just been through.

"Then make sure that bloody hairdresser doesn't **unleash** one of his trainees on me again!" she spat back.

There'll be minus points for that, I gloated to myself.

Shalima looked at Mona disapprovingly, but Mona just pushed past me and – just like me a few moments ago – disappeared behind the clothes rails (though not a lot was hanging on them by then, making them a rather **inadequate** screen). When someone took a photo with a flash, she got even angrier.

---

flair – Pfiff; to relish – genießen; braid – Zopf;
look lively – jetzt aber flott; to unleash – loslassen;
inadequate – unzulänglich

"Can you just **give** the **crap a break**?" she snapped at Ken. "Do you actually think anyone would buy your peeping Tom photos?"

The boys, who were now fully dressed, grinned and watched on **unashamedly**. Jost started to sing. *"Sex-bomb, sexbomb, you're my sexbomb ..."*

I thought that was really **below the belt**. They were just going too far. "Haven't you got anything else to do?" I had a go at them.

Ivo just grinned his head off. "Jealous are you?"

I could have strangled him. Why did every boy think I was jealous of Mona?

I grabbed Debbie and pulled her out into the backstage area. The show was about to begin anyway.

Ali put on *Miss California*, and Mrs Berger went onto the stage alone. She was also really well-dressed and was wearing a **snakeskin** trouser suit. Her bright red hair made a trendy contrast to her obvious elder years. "OK, so I'm an **old biddy**," she later admitted to me, "but an old biddy with **drive** and style! You girls have to get that far first!"

Ali **turned down** the music, and Mrs Berger welcomed the guests and explained that we were all non-professional models. Then she introduced the companies whose collections we'd be presenting. There were some really well-known names amongst them.

---

crap – Scheiß, Schrott; to give sth a break – mit etwas aufhören; unashamedly – ungeniert; below the belt – unter der Gürtellinie; snakeskin – Schlangenleder; old biddy – alte Oma; drive – Biss; to turn down – leise drehen

She thanked the perfume shop for the make-up and the hairdressing salon (don't make me laugh!) for the hairdos, and then things got rolling.

Ali turned up the music and the first group, led dynamically by Verena, came onto the catwalk.

She was greeted by friendly applause from the public and, as far as I could make out from between the partitions, everything looked like it was going perfectly. One girl after another came forward, walked down the long T, **gave a twirl** and came back into the line. Then they all went to the front together, and then went to the front in pairs. The whole group was dressed in beige and brown, and everything looked really harmonious. When the girls turned one last time to the public before leaving, they all smiled with satisfaction, happy that their premiere had gone so well.

And then we were on. Cindy, Mona, May and me. All of us in black and white. In contrast to her dark hair and to me, Mona was wearing a **wacky** white denim trouser suit dotted with glittering **rivets**. It didn't look too bad, I had to admit. But I was really satisfied with my own outfit, the **thorn** of envy didn't sit too deep in my side. Why couldn't I just completely forget about Mona? I sighed as I stepped out onto the catwalk. If only it was that easy.

Mrs Berger must have heard me sigh because she grabbed my arm and briefly held me back. "Smile, sweetie," she said encouragingly. "Show the world your teeth. You've got such a pretty smile!"

---

to give a twirl – sich drehen; wacky – abgefahren; rivet – Niete; thorn – Stachel

Then she must have missed my crooked canine tooth! But I still thought it was very nice of her to encourage me, and when the music started and Mona took the first step out onto the catwalk, I followed her feeling pretty **chirpy**.

But my mood soon changed dramatically when I looked out over the end of the catwalk. My God, where did all those people come from? My knees started to tremble, but I had to go on. Wasn't Mona scared of anything?

She strode off so **intrepidly**, it looked like she'd done nothing else all her life. I forced the **compulsory** smile onto my face and frantically tried to **keep up** with Mona until the end of the catwalk. When, **grinning like a Cheshire cat**, I looked out into the audience, I saw our three boys clapping and whistling from the **stationary** escalator. That's nice of them, I thought, and immediately started looking forward to performing with them. What really **threw** me, however, was a boy leaning against one of the columns. He was staring at me and looked completely **absorbed** in his thoughts. It was Meik. He really had come – even to my first show. I could hardly believe it.

I had to **tear myself away** from the sight of him be-

---

chirpy – beschwingt; intrepidly – beherzt;
compulsory – obligatorisch; to keep up – mithalten;
to grin like a Cheshire cat – wie ein Honigkuchenpferd grinsen;
stationary – still stehend, angehalten;
to throw sb – jmdn. durcheinander bringen;
absorbed – versunken; to tear oneself away – sich losreißen

cause Mona was already heading back. So I made my turn and **caught up** with her with two quick, unorthodox steps. "Stop walking so quickly," I hissed at her. We turned around again in the middle of the catwalk and took off our jackets. Then we threw them casually over our shoulders – Mona more casually than me, of course – and went back into line.

While the two other girls from our group walked up the catwalk, I couldn't help looking from Meik to Percy. They were just so different. How could I have fallen for both of them at the same time?

I was still thinking about this when we headed off again in a diagonal line, but I couldn't find an answer. It is the way it is, I thought and hummed along to the Jennifer Lopez hit which Ali had put on. *Love don't cost a thing*!

I finally **came to blows** with Mona while we were getting changed for the **penultimate** set. She didn't like the clothes she had to wear so – what did she do? – she just put on mine! She tried to claim it was all just a mistake, but I didn't believe her one minute.

"I'm really sorry, Shalima. I don't know how it happened."

The clock was ticking, and it was too late to do anything about it. Shalima said I had to go out in Mona's clothes. Her outfit had lots of beige parts which would

---

to catch up with sb – jmdn. einholen;
to come to blows – aneinander geraten;
penultimate – vorletzte

look really **dull** next to my blond hair. But my outfit, with its red top and funky trousers with a glitter **pattern**, made Mona a real **eye-opener**. Just you wait, I thought, I'll **get you back for** that.

The opportunity came straightaway when we performed with the boys. Mona was wearing a **wrap jacket** which was tied up at the back with a **ribbon**. To take the jacket off as quickly as possible during the presentation, the ribbon was tied with a very special **knot**. You could open it **in the blink of an eye**. While we were waiting backstage for our next cue, I just couldn't keep my fingers from tying together the two ends of the ribbons in another knot. And so, try as she might, Mona couldn't get the knot open and she **cut a** pretty **sorry figure** as she kept pulling at the ribbon, unable to accept the situation.

In the end, Ivo hissed, "Bloody hell, Mona, just leave the stupid thing alone. You're going to ruin the whole choreography!"

Of course, she thought that it was all my doing – at least that's how she looked at me. But she couldn't prove anything, and I washed my hands of it by saying sympathetically – and mainly for Shalima's ears – "What a shame, Mona, it almost ruined the whole choreography. You ought to check your things before the show more thoroughly. If you need help, just let me know."

---

dull – fade; pattern – Muster; eye-opener – Hingucker;
to get sb back for sth – es jmdm. heimzahlen;
wrap jacket – Wickeljacke; ribbon – Band; knot – Knoten;
in the blink of an eye – blitzschnell;
to cut a sorry figure – eine traurige Figur abgeben

If looks could kill, I would have been dead **on the spot**.

I was feeling pretty groggy before the finale. The constant getting changed was really exhausting. I'd brought a thin **silk scarf** with me which I put over my piled-up hair when I had to pull a new item of clothing over my head. The scarf saved my hairdo from being ruined. Shalima kept warning us not to get any make-up on our clothes – something which was easily done as we rushed to get changed.

For some reason all the stress backstage made me less nervous when I stepped out onto the catwalk. It was a relief to be walking in an orderly, **prearranged** manner and to escape the backstage chaos for a few minutes. I was immediately in a better mood as soon as I came onto the catwalk. And that meant my smile came more and more from inside, which **consequently** gave me the feeling that I was increasingly **appreciated** by the public. And when the audience responded to our big finale with a huge round of applause, I thought a good portion of that belonged to me.

"I want to become a model," I said to Debbie. "No question about it."

Even though I'd started to hate a whole load of people after the first day, I'd started to love modelling itself.

At home I made the mistake of euphorically telling Dad about the fashion show. He was paying us a **flying visit**,

---

on the spot – an Ort und Stelle; silk scarf – Seidentuch;
prearranged – vorgeplant; consequently – folglich;
to appreciate – schätzen; flying visit – Stippvisite

and in my **exuberance** I also unwisely expressed my desire to become a model. He inevitably saw it as his **paternal duty** to get "my feet back on the ground".

"If your mother **neglects** her duties as a parent so much," he **whinged**, "then I'll just have to set you some limits and give you a taste of reality. From now on you'll concentrate more on school. You'll need to get some decent qualifications when the time is right. So I want you to forget all about this fashion nonsense. You've got enough **brains** to get a decent job."

Huh, so my father was the **Big Chief**?!

In principle I had nothing against the course of my life which my dad had set for me. The only problem was that it wasn't mine. I had practically no say in it at all. You could hardly call that democratic. Needless to say, all he managed to do was provoke my **opposition**.

"OK, I'll do what you say," I said. "But then I want you to give up your job in Berlin, stop grumbling about your children, start a proper, middle-class job, spend every evening at home like every other father, play football with your son and help me with my homework."

That hit the mark. There was nothing he could say to that. I could tell he was angry that I'd caught him on his **Achilles heel**.

He threw his **napkin** onto the table, jumped up and

---

exuberance – Überschwang; paternal duty – väterliche Pflicht;
to neglect – vernachlässigen; to whinge – meckern;
brains – Grips; Big Chief – Oberhäuptling;
opposition – Widerstand; Achilles heel – Achillesferse;
napkin – Serviette

said somewhat too loudly, "OK then, do whatever you want, but as long as you eat at this table, you're not going to be a model! **Over my dead body**!"

Mum tried not to giggle, and the Joker snorted with laughter. "Do the two of you want to fight a duel?" he said. "Can I be the **second**?"

"Does anybody take me seriously in this house?" snapped Dad.

Mum shook her head cheekily, a grin on her face. "No, that's why you became a politician."

I **retired** to my room and called Franzi. "It's a shame you weren't there," I said with regret. "You really missed something special. It was **wicked**!"

And, without even thinking about how much the call was costing, I described everything that had happened, including Mona's bitchiness.

"... and you'll never guess who was there," I said at the end of my detailed report.

"Wölfchen!"

I giggled. "Almost ..." I said. "Mrs Ingrimm!"

"No, you're kidding me?"

I giggled even more because Franzi **fell for** my joke. "No, of course, it wasn't Mrs Ingrimm. Come on, guess."

But she had no idea, and so I told her with the **utmost** satisfaction, "Meik."

She was thrilled.

---

Over my dead body! – Nur über meine Leiche!;
second – Sekundant; to retire – sich zurückziehen;
wicked – (hier:) geil; to fall for sth – auf etwas reinfallen;
utmost – äußerst

"Really? I can't believe it. I thought he had a problem with fashion shows?! You can be proud of that. The boy must really like you."

It was pure **pleasure** hearing that at the end of my day!

But as I was lying in bed, I started to feel really **restless**. A horrible thought kept **gnawing** away at me: what if Meik hadn't come for me but because of the "mega-good-looking brunette" who squeezed up to him every morning in the bus? Perhaps the **rapt** look in his eyes hadn't been for me at all, but for her?

I had to speak to Franzi again.

"For crying out loud, girl!" she moaned. "I'm going to take away your license to call!"

"But it's a really terrible thought! I won't be able to **sleep a wink** tonight!"

"Aha, and so you want to **rob** me of my sleep as well, do you?"

"Do you think he only came because of Mona rather than me? Please, be honest!" I begged, ignoring her grumpy comments.

"Yes, I bet he did! He came because of Mona, and he thinks you're a complete **waste of space**! Which is just what I think! Goodnight!"

She just hung up on me!

I threw myself back onto my pillow and was **inwardly**

---

pleasure – Vergnügen; restless – unruhig; to gnaw – nagen;
rapt – versunken; to not sleep a wink – kein Auge zutun;
to rob – berauben;
waste of space – (hier:) zu nichts zu gebrauchen;
inwardly – seelisch

preparing myself for a night of **brooding** when my mobile phone peeped with an SMS.

*You looked beautiful. I'm jealous of any guy who gets the chance to set eyes upon you.*

*Meik*

Hm. So he really did come because of me. But it would be a lie to say I was over the moon about his SMS. Either he'd really fallen head over heels in love with me, or he had a problem: **over-the-top** jealousy!

---

to broode – brüten, grübeln; over-the-top – exzessiv

## Catwalk dreams

"Talk to him," Lea suggested the next morning at school. "Maybe he just picked the wrong words. You know, text messages often have a will of their own!"

But Franzi warned me, "There's nothing worse than jealous boys!" God knows how she knew that! But my girlfriends were right. I really had to find out if Meik's message was driven by his love for me or by his jealousy about the fashion show.

He just happened to turn up at the fashion show that afternoon. He was leaning against the same column, watching each and every one of my steps. At first I was really glad to see him, but when he was still standing around at the third performance, his presence started to get on my nerves. Being in love is all very well, but when you get the feeling that the guy is constantly keeping an eye on you, it's a real turn-off.

I decided to talk to him, as Lea had suggested. I tried to catch him twice after the show, but by the time I'd got changed, he'd already disappeared. Twice.

The most embarrassing thing was that other people were starting to notice him. When Percy **brought** him

---

to bring up sth – auf etwas ansprechen

**up** in the changing room, I just wanted to curl up and die.

"Is that your **bloke** or Mona's?" he asked. He'd obviously noticed that Meik **went** all **goggle-eyed** while watching our show.

It goes without saying that I seized the opportunity to **reduce** Mona's chances with Percy.

"I think he's Mona's boyfriend," I said with a cold smile. "At least, she always flirts with him in the schoolyard."

Got you! That really was a cool move. He'd probably lose interest in her now and would only have eyes for me.

As far as the competition was concerned, **ambition** had got me in its grasp in the meantime, and I hoped to get hold of that modelling contract. It was all Percy's fault that I'd started dreaming of the catwalk. He'd done quite a bit of modelling and was determined to start his professional career with this **event**.

"I'm going to win first prize here and then Mrs Berger won't be able to ignore me," he'd said casually a couple of days earlier while we were waiting to make our entrance. He grinned because I was looking at him so **incredulously**. "With your looks and charm you should think about doing the same," he said encouragingly. "There's no other job where you can make big money so quickly."

---

bloke – Macker; to go goggle-eyed – Glubschaugen machen;
to reduce – herabsetzen; ambition – Ehrgeiz;
event – Veranstaltung; incredulously – ungläubig

"You're pulling my leg," I replied.

But he shook his head. "No, not at all. You and Mona, you've both got a lot of charisma. The two of you could go far in this business."

I could have felt really flattered, but **my ears pricked up** at the sound of Mona's name. I was like one of **Pavlov's dogs** responding to a specifically trained stimulation, like a bell, for example, which **makes** the dog's **mouth water**. The **saliva** also started foaming up in my mouth when I heard her name. It was really awful the way she kept **competing** with me wherever I turned.

But still, Percy's words awoke hope in me. I was performing really well by then, certainly no worse than the others, and Mum confirmed this as I was drinking a quick **carrot juice** with her at the Juice Bar in a break between shows.

"You look really elegant and you move really well," she praised me, and my brother commented with his favourite vocabulary, "Really groovy!"

Mum had brought the Joker with her to the fashion show today, and I gave him the **task** of taking a good look at Percy so that he could give me his opinion afterwards.

"Well?" I asked as soon as I came through the door at home. "What do you think of him?"

---

to prick up one's ears – die Ohren spitzen;
Pavlov's dog – pawlowscher Hund; to make sb's mouth water – jmdm. das Wasser im Munde zusammenlaufen lassen;
saliva – Speichel; to compete – Konkurrenz machen;
carrot juice – Karottensaft; task – Aufgabe

"Absolutely funky-dorious!"

"And what does that mean in civilized English?"

"Not a bad guy. He's bound to make the glossy magazines."

"I don't want to know what you think of him as a model. I want to know what you think of him as a man."

The Joker got that speculative look in his eyes again. "I think he's cool. Isn't that enough?"

Yes, well, it wasn't exactly the ultimate **statement**, but the way he talked it was the closest you could get to a compliment.

"Three or four stars?" I asked to make sure I'd understood him properly.

"Four plus," he said generously. "Do you want to go out with him?"

Oh, my little brother! Why do elder sisters have to hear things like that?

Unfortunately, Franzi didn't like Percy. All she knew about him was through my effusive stories, and during a goodnight telephone call she tried to **talk me out of** him as best as she could.

"What is he? A student? And he wants to become a male model? What are you going to do with someone like him? Isn't he too old for you anyway? So how old is he then?"

"Nineteen. He's in his second **term**. So he's not stupid. Besides, he can study and model at the same time."

---

statement – Aussage;
to talk sb out of sth – jmdm. etwas ausreden; term – Semester

She fell silent.

"You just have to see him. Anyway, it's a **disgrace** that you haven't been to one single show yet with the *Pepper Dollies*!"

"That's true," admitted Franzi **remorsefully**. "But it's really difficult to find a date when we're all free at the same time. But I promise I'll see to it. You'll fall off the catwalk in surprise tomorrow when we all stand around it, bowling you over with our applause."

Her sudden show of enthusiasm must have **caught me unawares** because – although I actually wanted to keep it to myself – I unwisely confessed to her, "Listen, I've decided I want to become a model."

"I beg your pardon?" She was **thunderstruck**. "Did this Percy guy put that idea into your head? You can't be serious?"

"Why not? Mrs Berger said she's got a line of models who are fourteen and who perform in Berlin and Hamburg. They earn a thousand euros a day!"

Franzi was speechless for a moment on hearing this sum of money, but then she caught herself. "You're only thirteen, and you only earn that kind of money when you're the very best."

That hurt. "So, you don't reckon I can **make it big**! Well, that's no surprise: you've never seen me on the catwalk."

---

disgrace – Schande; remorsefully – reumütig;
to catch sb unawares – jmdn. überrumpeln;
thunderstruck – wie vom Donner gerührt;
to make it big – etwas Großes leisten

"I'll make up for it tomorrow," she conceded, "and then we can talk about the matter in more depth as far as I'm concerned."

I swallowed my anger. "OK. You really have to come though."

"I promise," said Franzi, and before she hung up, she gave me a **reminder**. "Don't forget: we've got an English test tomorrow."

Oh my giddy aunt! I'd completely forgotten about that. I rummaged my English book out of my school rucksack and tried to quickly learn a few grammar rules and some vocabulary, but in the end I couldn't keep my eyes open. I fell asleep over the book.

It was a **nightmare**! Miss-stress Ingrimm had once again packed a load of grammar into the English test, and after ten minutes I broke out into a sweat. If I became a model, then I wouldn't have to learn stupid vocabulary like this anymore, let alone know what a progressive form is!

My gaze **drifted** up from my exercise book to the window. The rain was beating against the **windowpane**, running down its face in long, wet trickles. Percy's face suddenly appeared on its surface like a slightly **blurred** mirror image in a **pond**.

"You really should become a model," he said in a soft voice. "We'll win the competition together and then start our careers!"

---

reminder – Hinweis; nightmare – Albtraum; to drift – schweifen; windowpane – Fensterscheibe; blurred – verschwommen; pond – Teich

That sounded so **tempting**. Our careers. What a romantic thought – to leave all of this behind me – the school, English tests, Mrs Ingrimm and Wölfchen – and to lead an exciting life with him as a model in the world's metropolises. A supermodel at his side, discovering Paris, Milan and New York ...

"Can I have your exercise book, please?" Mrs Ingrimm was standing next to me, holding her hand out for my test.

"But ... but I'm not finished yet," I stuttered, **struggling** to find my way out of my catwalk dreams back into the **dreary** reality of the classroom.

"That's bad luck, I'm afraid. The bell has already rung. I can't give you any more time, unfortunately."

I closed my exercise book feeling frustrated and handed it to her. I bet it was a real mess.

I unexpectedly crossed paths with Meik at lunch break. As he stood close in front of me, I remembered what I thought was so great about him: that **unruly** blond hair of his, those big blue eyes and ... oh, he just looked cool!

But what he said wasn't cool at all. "You just live for your fashion show now, do you?!"

"What makes you think that?" I asked in a slightly unfriendly tone because his question had sounded like a **reproach**.

"The only time I get to see you is on the catwalk," he explained.

---

tempting – verlockend; to struggle – kämpfen; dreary – trist, öde; unruly – widerspenstig; reproach – Vorwurf

I thought of Lea's words: talk to him …

"We can meet up another time if that's not enough for you," I said and – paff! – I was saddled with a date.

"OK, let's say a time and place now." He didn't let the opportunity slip through his fingers this time. "How about going to the cinema tonight? Are you allowed to go to the 10 o'clock **screening**?"

Are you allowed! I probably wasn't allowed, but Mum had a meeting out of town tonight and would probably be home around midnight. If I **bribed** the Joker with a junior bag of junk food from McBurger, he'd keep his mouth shut. So I accepted Meik's suggestion, and he said goodbye with a big smile on his face.

"So, see you at the Cinemaxx this evening then. Ciao, Kiki."

My name had sounded really nice coming from his lips. Almost as nice as Percy's "Ciao, bella!"

That afternoon Franzi did, in fact, come to the show with the *Pepper Dollies*. Meik, however, didn't turn up. It looked like it was enough for him to see me in the evening.

As I came into the changing room, I saw Percy leaning over Mona's shoulder. It looked like he was **burying** his face in her long, dark hair. They must have heard me coming in because they shot apart and he pretended to be helping her do up her top. I stared at the two of them furiously. Was something really going on between them?

---

screening – Vorstellung; to bribe – bestechen;
to bury – vergraben

In the course of the shows I'd developed a special relationship with modelling. I didn't want to be a walking clothes stand, as Meik had described it so **derogatorily**. I had developed a game in which I played a role which matched the clothes I was wearing.

And it worked. As soon as I stepped out into the **spotlights,** I could really get the audience to see the person in me who I wanted to be. It was a most satisfying feeling. If I was wearing an ordinary outfit with jeans and a T-shirt, for example, then I imagined being Mum's "girl next door". If I was wearing a long **evening gown** and "big hair", I pretended to be a lady from the world of the rich and famous, and I carried myself with stylish finesse!

Oh, I was so rich and beautiful!

For the second set of the day I slipped into a very **skimpy**, pink sleeveless top and grey and pink **ringed** trousers. As a finishing touch I wore a green snakeskin jacket. It really looked straight out of a fashion magazine, but it **took some getting used to**. When I'd first seen the outfit hanging on the clothes stand, I'd wanted to turn around and run away. No respectable person could wear something like that. I felt like the hottest thing in town.

But there was no point complaining! The clothes had to go out onto the catwalk. I then realised why only people with a healthy self-confidence could become models. Hey, everyone, look at me, the things I'm wearing may

---

derogatorily – abwertend; spotlight – Scheinwerfer;
evening gown – Abendkleid; skimpy – knapp; ringed – geringelt;
to take getting used to – gewöhnungsbedürftig sein

be really **crass**, but aren't I still the most beautiful of them all?

"Come on, move it! Get into your clothes!" Shalima **urged** us. "Stop being so **prim**! You've got no idea about fashion! People in Berlin walk around the streets dressed like this. Just forget your provincial taste."

When it was time to go out onto the catwalk, I really had to make an effort to come up with an idea of who I could be. In the end, I decided to be Britney Spears – clean and **aloof** despite the provocative **belly button** on display.

The applause from the audience proved I'd been right in my decision. My friends also clapped enthusiastically. I was obviously quite a talented actor.

Everything would have been just fine if Mona hadn't **unintentionally** changed the choreography again. Instead of going back into the middle with me after making the last turn together, she just strode back to the front of the catwalk, put her leather jacket back on, and strolled to the exit with a big smile on her face. **To cap it all** she turned around again in front of the exit and tossed her hair back to a special applause.

Shalima was so busy noting down the points that she hadn't spotted any of this. "Why are you hanging around here again?" she had a go at me suddenly. "Did you take your exit too early, or what? Just be more careful next time."

---

crass – krass; to urge – drängen; prim – zimperlich;
aloof – distanziert; belly button – Bauchnabel;
unintentionally – unabsichtlich; to cap it all – zu allem Überfluss

That really was the limit! Mona did what she wanted and I got a **dressing-down**. But, as I'd already found out, there was absolutely no point protesting to Shalima. She just took off points for bad sportsmanship.

"That silly cow Mona," I cursed. "She'd better watch out. Otherwise I'll give her a **taste of her own medicine**."

"Are you thinking of anything **in particular**?" Debbie asked curiously.

I shrugged my shoulders. "We'll see." I'd think of something **nasty** enough.

I was surprised to hear Percy giving me his support.

"You can't let her get away with that," he said. "I'd **put a damper on** her if I were you. She already thinks she's the winner."

Well, she couldn't be sure of that yet. There were a few other people with their sights on first prize as well.

Just before our next performance Mona couldn't find her shoes. She looked for them all over the place and got herself worked up into a real state. She almost broke down in tears at the thought of not being able to perform. Shalima **gave her a good talking-to** because everybody was responsible for their own things.

"What can I do about it if someone steals my shoes?" she tried to justify herself, but she only made things

---

dressing-down – Anschiss; to give sb a taste of one's own medicine – es jmdm. mit gleicher Münze heimzahlen;
in particular – etwas Bestimmtes; nasty – fies;
to put a damper on sb – jmdm. einen Dämpfer aufsetzen;
to give sb a good talking-to – jmdm. eine Standpauke halten

worse because all the other girls felt Mona was pointing her finger at them.

I was glad to have to go onto the catwalk. It was a particular pleasure this time around. Instead of having to perform with bitchy Mona, I was with sweet Percy, who'd quickly **jumped in** for her.

I wore a dress for the first time. **Ankle-length** and very **tight-fitting** – and that without a Wonderbra!!!

"Aren't I too young for that?" I'd asked Mrs Berger hesitantly.

But she'd just said, "Who cares about your age?! Elegance, darling! For a dress like that you need to have the **poise** of a princess, and you've got just that. Shoulders back and off you go!!"

And on the steps Percy whispered to me, "I've got an idea. It'll get us loads of points. Just leave it to me!"

OK, then!

We really did get a huge round of applause because at the end Percy **swirled** me around like a Tango dancer, pulled me up tight to him, bent my **torso** back and gave me a kiss on the lips. God, the blood just rushed to my head. The make-up artist's rouge was completely superfluous! It was great that my friends were there that day and could **witness** this triumph. If Franzi still didn't think Percy was as great as I did, then she was obviously suffering from a serious lack of taste!

Whoever had made Mona's shoes disappear – I was

---

to jump in – einspringen; ankle-length – knöchellang; tight-fitting – eng; poise – Haltung; to swirl – herumwirbeln; torso – Oberkörper; to witness – mit ansehen

eternally thankful to him. Of course, Debbie thought I had done it, but my conscience was as clear as if it had just been washed with Ariel.

"It wasn't me. Honest," I protested.

After **replacement** shoes had been brought over for Mona, we then found out that someone had thrown the old pair into the bin.

"Probably the **cleaning lady**," said Miss Dreary-Face Cindy with a rather **sanctimonious** tone in her voice – which made me think that she might be the real **culprit** herself. Obviously, I wasn't the only one who saw an unwanted competitor in Mona. Which meant that I'd have to keep my eyes open myself over the next few days.

After the last show I went for a quick carrot juice with my friends. We were standing at a table in the Juice Bar when Percy and Ivo strolled past us.

"Ciao, bella!" called Percy, and it was an inner pleasure to see all the *Pepper Dollies* turn around to look at him.

"I can understand you," said Lea. "He's really gorgeous. Top quality!"

Franzi, however, still had her reservations about Percy, and she thought it necessary to remind me about Meik straightaway. "What about him? Do you want to leave him to Mona? Lea saw him with her in the bus today. They were chatting away about the fashion show."

"Yes, he gave her some really sweet compliments!" **recalled** Lea.

---

replacement – Ersatz; cleaning lady – Putzfrau;
sanctimonious – scheinheilig; culprit – Schuldiger;
to recall – sich erinnern

Needless to say, I was hardly thrilled to hear this piece of news. Just because I had **pushed** Mona **out of** Percy's **favour** today, didn't mean I wanted to leave Meik to her. After all, the two of them came into my final selection and, as long as I couldn't decide on one of them, she should leave her **paws** off him.

"Well, I'm going to the cinema tonight with Meik," I said and astonished my friends with this piece of news. "I'll **grill** him about what he thinks of Mona." And to myself I thought, I'll grill him till he burns if necessary.

But it wasn't necessary. When I met up with Meik in the Cinemaxx, he already had popcorn and tickets. I was so excited I forgot to ask him what film we were seeing. It was the 10 o'clock show, and the whole thing started with an impressive laser show. The room filled with smoke, and I suddenly had a really bad **coughing fit** just in the middle of one of the nicest 3D effects. I thought I was going to choke on my popcorn. It would have been a tragic end to a romance that had only just begun!

Meik slapped me timidly on the back, but that didn't help at all. I huffed and **puffed** until the tears rolled down my face. I just wanted to curl up and die, it was so embarrassing.

I must have groaned really loudly because Meik put his arm around me to comfort me and whispered, "Don't

---

to push sb out of sb's favour – jmdn. bei jmdm. ausstechen; paws – Pfoten; to grill sb – jmdm. auf den Zahn fühlen; coughing fit – Hustenanfall; to puff – keuchen

worry, it's not so bad. You probably just choked on the popcorn, didn't you?"

Exhausted, I leant against his shoulder and closed my eyes. The stream of tears soon dried up, the smoke dispersed and the film began. But – my head remained on his shoulder, his arm held me safe and **sound**.

At some point I felt his fingers running softly through my hair. His hand was warm and I liked its touch. I felt really warm and safe and I started to forget about everything. I felt like a big pink marshmallow. And then Meik started **nibbling** at me.

After that I have no idea what happened in the film. I don't know how it ended and I don't know how I got home afterwards. My last memory was a **hug** at the garden **fence** and a long goodbye kiss.

When I turned off my bedside lamp, two questions came into my head before I fell into a deep sleep: Was I now together with Meik? And what about Percy? I felt really bad about things. It just wasn't on to be in love with two boys at the same time!

"Hormones, nothing but hormones!" said Franzi precociously when I told the *Pepper Dollies* about the problem the next day. "Why should boys be the only ones troubled by hormones?"

Oh no! I really wasn't the type to be a hormonal slave. Where was the romance? Goddesses of fate spinning their **threads** was much more poetic than the hormonal

---

sound – (hier:) fest; to nibble – naschen; hug – Umarmung; fence – Zaun; thread – Faden

theory introduced in Biology. Even the little **winged** guy with his **bow and arrow** was better than that.

"Feelings come from the soul," Lea backed me up. "You can't reduce them to a biological process. Love is a lot, lot more."

Exactly. The girl was right. Hormones, that sounded sterile and aseptic, and no matter what love really was, I knew from my own experience that it wasn't sterile and aseptic. Maybe in glossy magazines it was, but not in real life. Not when a real boy meets a real girl.

"Oh, by the way ..." Franzi's thirst for information wasn't satisfied yet. "Did you finally kiss?"

"No, we **twiddled our thumbs**!" I said. The *Pepper Dollies* stared at me in bewilderment. "Of course, we kissed," I added with a giggle.

"And? How was it?"

"**Wet**."

Franzi was disappointed.

"That doesn't sound very romantic."

"No, it wasn't really," I confessed. "It was a bit of a **slobber** match," I added frankly.

"Oh my giddy aunt!" groaned Greetje.

All the *Pepper Dollies* started giggling with embarrassment. They obviously thought a French kiss would be a bit different. Me, too, actually.

"Was it so bad?" said Lea **compassionately**.

"What do you mean, bad? It was ... no ... it wasn't

---

winged – mit Flügeln; bow and arrow – Pfeil und Bogen;
to twiddle one's thumbs – Däumchen drehen; wet – nass;
to slobber – sabbern; compassionately – voller Mitgefühl

bad. It … it was … " I tried to find the right word, but it wasn't at all easy to describe the unfamiliar feeling of kissing Meik without making it sound **mundane**. It wasn't mundane at all. It was special. But at the same time it wasn't the dream that's promised in books and magazines.

"Hm," I said in the end to my **expectant** friends. "I can't describe it. It was surprising and different and nice and also a bit … er … well … wet. But it got better after a while …"

I stopped talking. Jeepers, what was I **babbling** on about?

Franzi immediately drew her conclusions from my verbal **clumsiness**. "The way you talk, he doesn't sound like Mr Right to me!"

What now? Him neither? First of all she **spoiled** Percy for me and now Meik as well?

But Lea said, "Perhaps you just have to practise kissing. Everybody thinks you fall in love, kiss and that's it. Everything's perfect. But maybe it's different. Maybe even kissing **calls for** practice."

There was a lot to support this opinion. After all, as time passed, I'd had the feeling that it was much better between me and Meik. And the goodbye kiss at the garden fence wasn't too bad at all.

Just thinking about this must have conjured up the look of love on my face because Lea suddenly said, "Well,

---

mundane – profan; expectant – erwartungsvoll;
to babble – plappern; clumsiness – Ungeschicklichheit;
to spoil – madig machen; to call for – (hier:) erfordern

it can't have all been that bad yesterday. You look really in love!"

I sighed and felt myself turning red. "Meik's sweet. He really is ..."

Time flew by, and it was soon the penultimate day of the fashion show. People were getting themselves ready for the end. Despite the fact that we were all **competing** hotly for points to win the competition, most of us thought it was a shame everything would soon be over.

"It's a shame," I said to Debbie. "We won't see each other every day anymore."

Debbie nodded.

"I'm really going to miss the fashion show, believe me," she admitted. "I've **got** so **used to** it. I'll probably be really bored without it."

She said exactly what I was thinking. The fashion show had given my normal everyday life a real kick. I wondered if something like this could be **addictive** – the chic clothes, glamour, make-up, and **ingenious** hairdressers? Would my life feel completely empty when all of that was gone? No more fantastic styling, no more big performances, no more audience and no more applause? I'd definitely miss all the compliments from the boys. Maybe even the bitchiness amongst the other girls. I mean, who could I make disparaging remarks about without Miss Horse-Face and Miss Dreary-Face?

---

to compete – wetteifern;
to get used to sth – sich an etwas gewöhnen;
addictive – süchtig machen; ingenious – ideenreich

"Do you think you and Percy have got a future?" asked Debbie. "After all, he did kiss you in public."

Unfortunately, I couldn't answer that question either. Certainly not after the previous evening. After all, Percy wasn't the only boy who'd kissed me. It was too bad I'd have to decide on one of them so soon!

I pushed this horrible thought out of my mind as Jost said, "Hey, girls, are you joining us? We want to go for a **farewell** drink. Everybody will go their separate ways tomorrow."

He was probably right there. I couldn't imagine that all the people who *hadn't* won a prize were going to celebrate.

"Where are you going?" I asked.

"To Meier's beer garden, and after that who knows."

Mum wasn't at home that evening, and grandma was looking after the Joker. If I gave her a quick call on my mobile, then I could probably go out with them for a bit.

I imagined it was the last chance for me to finally win over Percy. After all, he lived here in town, and there was nothing against us being together after the fashion show was over. Maybe it would be the start of a fantastic career together!

"What do you reckon, shall we join them?" Debbie sounded like she was **up for it**.

"Is Mona coming, too?" I asked Jost.

"Yeah, of course, she is," he said. "Everybody's coming."

Well, in that case! And to myself I secretly hoped to

---

farewell – Abschied; to be up for sth – unternehmungslustig

find the answer to my question as the evening went on: who was the right one for me, Percy or Meik? But to find out for sure, Percy would have to kiss me one more time!

And he'd have to do it properly this time – not just for show!

The evening in the beer garden was really good fun until it cooled off and somebody suggested we change bars. Some wanted to go to Salambo, others to the Harlequin, and some to Mmex.

"Well, then I'm going to go home," I said. "I can't get into a disco anyway."

But the boys thought **otherwise**. "Of course, you can get in. They'll let you in for sure if you go with us."

And with a **look of appraisal** Percy added, "With all that make-up you look much older than sixteen. And once you're in no one will check you anyway."

I wasn't so sure myself, and I thought the whole thing sounded very **risky**. So I decided to wait until I found out what Mona was doing.

She glanced across at me as Percy asked her. I expect she was thinking the same as me. It was probably the last opportunity to win over Percy for both of us, and neither of us wanted to let the other get away with it.

"I'll come with you," said Mona, and I quickly called over half the table, "Me, too!"

So we went to the Harlequin. It was the trendiest disco in town and well-known for its lax controls. It really was

---

otherwise – anders; look of appraisal – abschätzender Blick; risky – gewagt no problem to get past the **bouncers**. They were only keeping an eye out for people who had been **banned** because they'd **gone on the rampage**, dealt drugs or had been caught stealing.

Percy bought me a **shandy** and, although there was only a bit of alcohol in it, it put me in a really good mood and I soon **loosened up**.

Whenever music came on which had been in the fashion show, the whole clique rushed onto the dance floor and danced like crazy.

Percy was clever enough to sometimes dance with me and sometimes with Mona.

"Man, that's really crass," I said to Debbie. "Sometimes her, sometimes me. Which of us do you think he likes the most?"

"It's difficult to say," Debbie admitted with a grin. "But one thing's for sure: she fancies him just as much as you do!"

I just had him to myself again when someone suddenly touched my arm. I looked around and let go of Percy **with a start**.

Standing next to me was none other than Meik! Crikey, where did he come from? He'd turned up on the dance floor out of the blue. I was completely taken aback. But then I remembered that he was already sixteen and probably went in and out of this disco. What bad luck it was that he had to be here today of all days. That didn't

---

bouncers – Türsteher; banned – Hausverbot haben;
to go on a rampage – Randale machen; shandy – Radler;
to loosen up – locker werden; with a start – erschrocken

suit me at all. If he made a scene with me now! That would probably turn Percy completely off!

Meik didn't make a scene, but he **insisted** I talk to him alone.

"Listen, I'll be right back," I said to Percy, feeling uncomfortable. "I just have to deal with something here."

Percy grinned suggestively and said, "Aha, deal with who? Not Mona's boyfriend?"

Damn it. He'd seen through my lie. He'd probably **launch himself at** Mona as soon as I was out of sight.

But when I turned around again, I saw him dancing with Miss Dreary-Face Cindy. There you go, I thought in relief. She's not dangerous to me at all!

I let Meik drag me over to a corner behind the bar.

He asked me if I wanted a Coke, and I turned him down grumpily.

"What do you want?" I asked. "Can't you see I'm with friends here?"

"But you're not sixteen," he said. "You're not allowed to be in here."

"Could you say that a bit louder perhaps?" I hissed at him indignantly and looked around. Hopefully no one had heard his indiscreet remark. "Are you trying to **blackmail** me?"

He looked unhappy. "Do you really think I'd do a thing like that?" And with a sad look in his eyes like a dog he added, "Didn't you like it yesterday evening?"

---

to insist – auf etwas bestehen;
to launch oneself at sb – sich auf jmdn. stürzen;
to blackmail – erpressen

Oh, **spare** me, please. Don't play the **softy** again!

"Yes, of course, I liked it," I said and added **mischievously**, "especially the film!"

"Look, why don't you just come out with it? Tell me you don't like me to my face!" He'd drawn his conclusions quickly.

For crying out loud! What was I meant to say to that? I really wasn't in the mood to have a deep and **meaningful** conversation about our relationship. I didn't have the **crucial** information which I urgently needed from Percy.

"Listen, I like you a lot, and something could really become of us, but this evening I'm here with the people from the fashion show and it's our last evening and I want to spend it with them. That's got nothing to do with you and me."

He still didn't look satisfied. He looked at his watch and said, "It's almost midnight. Don't you have to go home? I could walk you back."

That was really very nice of him, but I wanted to stay. At least as long as Mona was here. That's what I told him.

"You really should go," he said, trying to **scare** me. "This place is checked after midnight. They'll throw you out then anyway. Everybody under eighteen has to go. Me, too."

"Oh, I bet they don't look that closely!" I dismissed his **objection**.

---

to spare – verschonen; softy – Sensibelchen;
mischievously – spitzbübisch; meaningful – bedeutsam;
crucial – entscheidend; to scare – Angst machen;
objection – Einwand

When he noticed that I wasn't going to **budge,** he couldn't hold himself back. "Come on, just admit you only want to stay because of the guy from the fashion show!" he **blurted out**. "He's been coming on to you all evening."

Now it was my turn to be thunderstruck. How jealous could anyone be?! What had Franzi said? There's nothing worse than jealous boys? I really had to agree with her there.

And feeling absolutely livid I replied, "Go and look for a **guard dog** you can **chain up** – I'm just not the type for that!"

I tossed my head back, pulled back my shoulders and strutted off with my best modelling walk – in the role of the **offended** diva! "My kingdom is only worth a king, and you ..." I hummed to myself, "... you're not kingly enough!"

---

not to budge – stur bleiben; to blurt out – herausplatzen;
guard dog – Kettenhund; to chain up – anketten;
offended – beleidigt

## Love don't cost a thing

After all this stress it was more **pressing** than ever that I made my decision. Plucking up my courage after a second shandy, I decided to get to work. Now or never!

I was just about to throw myself at Percy when the music suddenly stopped and the lights went on. Complete chaos broke out. I looked at my watch. It was just after midnight.

"This place is **swarming with** police," someone shouted, and the DJ confirmed the bad news. In an attempt to keep the mood **upbeat** he called into the microphone: "Let's give the law a warm welcome!"

A few people clapped, others made jokes. One or the other started to get nervous.

"Great," said a boy who also wasn't eighteen. "I've always wanted to go to the police station!"

His **black humour** disappeared, however, as soon as the seriousness of the situation became clear. **Plain clothed** and uniformed police officers were appearing all over the place, asking people for their identity cards. Well,

---

pressing – dringlich;
to be swarming with sth – von etwas wimmeln; upbeat – fröhlich;
black humour – Galgenhumor; plain clothed – in Zivil

I thought, that's just great. They're going to have a really good laugh when they take a look at my kiddy-card.

The boy next to me now started to panic. "They're going to take us all with them," he shrieked and tried to get to the exit where one of the officers immediately grabbed him.

I now also started looking for a way to escape. And Debbie started moaning next to me. "What are we going to do now? How are we going to get out of this?"

A girl who also didn't look very old was playing it cool. She emptied her bottle of beer down her throat.

"This is ridiculous!" she said with a **wobbly** voice. "They can't possibly arrest everyone here."

But they could. And they did.

I stared at the growing queue of people who had to register themselves at a table of the **Youth Department**.

"Can we go when the people from the Youth Department have written down our names?" Debbie and I wanted to know.

Jost shook his head **gravely**. "I don't think so. I think we all have to go to the police station first. Your parents can pick you up there."

I felt like I'd just **accidentally** landed under a **fairground** hammer. My head began to pound as if a storm was going on inside it. Oh God, what would Mum say? And – even worse – Dad? He mustn't get to know about it!

---

wobbly – wackelig; Youth Department – Jugendamt;
gravely – ernst; accidentally – versehentlich;
fairground – Rummelplatz

But my wish didn't come true. The policewoman checking my ID stared at me and said, "Well, well, if it isn't Kristina Siebert? Aren't you the daughter of the Member of Parliament? I saw a photo of your family in the newspaper a few days ago."

Oh no! Not that too. Didn't I have a bad feeling at the time of that photo session?!

The policewoman obviously didn't vote for my dad's party because her tone of voice wasn't exactly friendly when she said, "Isn't your father an expert on youth policies? He'll be happy to have to pick you up at the police station!"

Debbie **clung** to me. She was crying her eyes out and her make-up was running in thick streams down her face.

In the meantime the mood had swung. The air was **stuffy** and tense with aggression.

A group of **rowdy** guys started to go on the rampage and throw beer bottles against the wall. The police quickly **clamped down** on them and led them away. "Keep cool, mate. Hands off!" said the leader **snottily** as a policeman grabbed his arm. "Nice and slowly. I'm coming." He could hardly walk in a straight line, so he must have been pretty drunk, and he obviously didn't realise fully what was going on.

I heard a policewoman next to me sigh. "This is a kindergarten here. We'll never get them all over to the station."

"They might let a few of us go," I whispered to Deb-

---

to cling – klammern; stuffy – stickig; rowdy – rüpelhaft;
to clamp down – scharf vorgehen; snottily – patzig

bie full of hope. "They can't possibly have enough space at the police station for all these people."

But my hope was **short-lived**. We were all taken to a police van and it was off to the next station.

Oh, the disgrace of it all! They really were going to put us **behind bars**! I just wanted the earth to open up and swallow me!

I got put in a small cell with a lot of other girls.

We had to give the police our parents' telephone numbers, and then the police started to call around.

Those of us who had a mobile phone and were gutsy enough now tried to reach their parents themselves and tell them the bad news.

After about ten minutes the first worried parents arrived and a few girls could leave the cell. That was good because **reinforcements** soon came, and I **reconciled** myself with my fate slightly when I saw a familiar face: Mona.

Well, at least she hadn't got away.

She sat down on a **plank bed** as far away from me as possible and stared ahead in silence. As more and more girls were picked up, the mood became more optimistic as well. Someone even **dared** to make the odd joke or two.

Most of the parents dealt with the situation fairly coolly.

"Why do you have to kick up such a fuss?" one of the

---

short-lived – kurzlebig; behind bars – hinter Gitter; reinforcements – Nachschub; to reconcile – versöhnen; plank bed – Pritsche; to dare – wagen

mothers asked a policewoman. "My daughter's turning eighteen in two weeks anyway. She's been going to the Harlequin almost every weekend since her sixteenth birthday. You'd be better off making sure the owners didn't give the kids alcohol at their free-beer parties!"

There were, on the other hand, parents who reacted much more aggressively. They gave their daughters a good shouting at, threatening to **ground** them and stop their pocket money. They complained about how annoying it was having to pick their daughter up from a police station in the middle of the night.

Needless to say, there wasn't one single Member of Parliament amongst the various parents or **guardians**. Particularly not one whose daughter had just ruined his election campaign as I had done. No punishment could be bad enough to make that good …

One girl after another was picked up and, after Debbie was called out, I felt really alone.

I hope Mum isn't still with her **clients** in Hanover, I thought. If she'd turned off her mobile phone, then I might end up **rotting away** here! I couldn't bother Grandma with all this. She'd smell Sodom and Gomorrah straightaway. She had a weak heart, and there was no way I could risk getting her all worked up. Besides, she was probably fast asleep and was **as deaf as a post** anyway.

And then everyone had gone. All of them except me and – Mona.

---

to ground sb – jmdm. Hausarrest geben;
guardian – Erziehungsberechtigter; client – Kunde;
to rot away – verfaulen; deaf as a post – stocktaub sein

I really don't know if my crime deserved a punishment as bad as this. I mean, I wasn't in here for murder!

She was still sitting on the plank bed at one end of the cell, and I was at the other. We were staring at the floor to avoid looking at each other.

It was a really stupid situation.

"What a pain," I said in the end, just to break the silence. "My dad's going to kill me!"

"At least I'll be rid of you then!" she said with a grin.

Did I just hear right? She really had a nerve! Even in this situation she was as cheeky as dog shit!

"Don't get your hopes up," I said. "My mum might have something to say about that. And my brother, too."

"Is your brother that **gnome**? The one who always hangs around with you in break?"

"My brother's not a gnome!" I **stuck up for** the Joker. "Don't you have any brothers or sisters?"

She shook her head. "No, I'm spared all that. But instead I've got a **single mum** on my back. She's hanging around at some reception right now while her daughter's rotting away in the **nick**."

She's going through the same as me, I thought, and was once again surprised at how many similarities there were between us. We both fell silent.

Something clicked and **crackled** in the cell and the light began to **flicker**. It was really **nerve-racking**.

---

gnome – Gartenzwerg; to stick up for sb –
sich für jmdn. einsetzen; single mum – allein erziehende Mutter;
nick – Knast; to crackle – knacken; to flicker – flackern;
nerve-racking – nervtötend

"The bulb's going to blow any moment." Mona stared at the light.

"Do you think our parents are going to get into trouble with Youth Department? You know, for **abusing** their **parental responsibility** and all that?"

Mona shrugged her shoulders. "No idea. But they can't **employ** a babysitter for all of us twenty-four hours a day."

I sighed. "My dad would."

All of a sudden, Mona started to giggle. "But he's a politician. Maybe next time he can **lend** you one of his bodyguards!"

"If he's good-looking, why not?" I giggled as well and pictured a muscular bodyguard with Percy's sweet face.

Percy! I glanced disapprovingly at Mona. She was still my rival. Our shared time in the nick hadn't changed that. She wanted to win the competition – as well as Percy – just as much as I did!

A thought flashed through my head: perhaps I could speak to her openly about the situation? It couldn't do any **harm**. After all, tomorrow – I mean, today – was the fashion show, and Percy would have to choose between the two of us.

"Hm, listen, Mona? About Percy …"

She looked **wide awake** all of a sudden. Her exhaustion was replaced by a **tense expectancy**.

---

to abuse – verletzen; parental responsibility – Aufsichtspflicht;
to employ – beschäftigen; to lend – leihen; harm – Schaden;
wide awake – hellwach;
tense expectancy – erwartungsvolle Spannung

I **faltered** and started again. "Listen, about Percy ... do you fancy him or what?" There – it was out.

Mona remained silent. How could she **keep me in suspense** like this?

"I mean, have you fallen in love with him?"

"Have *you*?"

That was mean to answer a question with a question. Couldn't she just put her cards on the table? I shivered because it was pretty cold in the cell – not just because of my mood. I wanted to go home. I wanted to be in my warm, cosy bed. I picked up the **thread of conversation** again to finally get a clear picture.

"Well, as far as I'm concerned," I started hesitantly, overcoming my **reluctance**. "I've got a certain interest."

Mona looked at the floor and drew imaginary lines and circles with her foot. Then she seemed to pull herself together. "Me, too," she admitted. "He's the most amazing boy I've ever met."

That's exactly what I'd feared.

"I think so, too," I said, slightly embarrassed.

"But he really fancies me," Mona suddenly claimed with a self-confidence that remained **undiminished**.

"Aha, you think so?!" Her claim had taken me by surprise, and I fell silent for a moment. After a while I added, "He gave me the same feeling."

Silence. I took the initiative again. "I think it's about time he made a decision, don't you? You or me."

---

to falter – stocken; to keep sb in suspense – jmdn. zappeln lassen; thread of conversation – Gesprächsfaden; reluctance – Abneigung; undiminished – unvermindert

Mona nodded and grinned mischievously. "Then we should just ask him."

On a sudden **wave** of **rationality** and goodwill I decided that this was a really good idea. And so we agreed to put a gun to his head the next day.

"He's been **playing** us **off** against each other long enough. He has to decide now."

Mona seemed almost relaxed – if not exhausted – after having come to this agreement. She yawned. "Shall we **bury the hatchet**?" she asked, stretching herself out on the bench.

Now listen to that! But after all the horrid things that had happened on the catwalk, I couldn't trust the way she was suddenly waving the **white flag**. How could I tell she wasn't already planning something mean to **trick** me at the last minute in the fashion show competition?

"We could try," I said – purely for tactical reasons – and decided to be even more **on my guard**. And to **lull her** a bit **into a false sense of security** I added, "By the way, it wasn't me who stole your shoes – maybe you should keep an eye on Cindy."

I must have **nodded off** because I was woken up by loud steps and **scraps of conversation**. To my indescribable

---

wave – Anwandlung; rationality – Vernunft;
to play off – ausspielen;
to bury the hatchet – das Kriegsbeil begraben;
white flag – Friedensfahne; to trick – austricksen;
to be on one's guard – auf der Hut sein; to lull sb into a false sense of security – jmdm. in falscher Sicherheit wiegen;
to nod off – einnicken; scraps of conversation – Wortfetzen

delight I saw two women standing in front of the prison cell accompanied by a policewoman. One of the women was my mother. The policewoman opened up and I rushed into my mum's arms.

The other woman was **instantly** recognisable. She was obviously Mona's mum. They had a lot of similarities. She was wearing business clothes and looked very **well-groomed**. Hm, I really could imagine her in a first-class restaurant. As if she had read my thoughts, Mona grinned at me. Back to her old self.

"See you around!" she said as we left. "Don't forget our deal!"

How could I?! After all, my entire happiness was **dependent on** it.

As I was sitting in the car, I suddenly realised with a shock that I hadn't asked Mona about Meik. I really wanted to know what went on between them every morning on the bus. But I didn't have any time to think about it because Mum started having a go at me as soon as I was in the car. She really made the wildest reproaches. She was particularly annoyed that, if things came out into the open, then I'd have given Dad's **opponents** some real **dynamite** in the middle of the election campaign.

Needless to say, my identity didn't remain a secret.

Dad **went ape-shit**. Every morning in Berlin he read the local newspaper from his constituency, so he found

---

instantly – sofort; well-groomed – gepflegt;
to be dependent on – abhängig von; opponent – Gegner;
dynamite – Zündstoff; to go ape-shit – ausrasten

out first thing the next day. As a Youth Politician there was no way he could overlook the front-page **headline**:

*Midnight sting in **hornets' nest** – 13-year-olds caught **red-handed** in the disco. In a special operation police hold daughter of MP Siebert!*

Just fantastic, I thought as I saw the newspaper. As a VIP girl you got an extra kick up the backside. Why wasn't my father just a **vacuum cleaner salesman** or a **wandering preacher**?

I was just glad it was a Saturday and there was no school today. Wölfchen would have probably given me a complete dressing-down. Fashion show and disco – I don't think he could have coped with that. At least on Monday I could tell him the good news that my "nightmare fashion show" had finally come to an end and promise him **from the bottom of my heart** that I would never again smuggle myself into a disco before my sixteenth birthday.

Needless to say, my dad **hit the roof**.

"I wanted to stay in Berlin and work at the weekend, but this calls for a family conference," he **barked** down the phone after Mum forced me to take his call. He was so **curt** with me, I feared the worst. "I'm coming home this evening on the 6 o'clock train."

---

headline – Schlagzeile; hornets' nest – Wespennest;
red-handed – auf frischer Tat; vacuum cleaner salesman – Staubsaugervertreter; wandering preacher – Wanderprediger;
from the bottom of my heart – von ganzem Herzen;
to hit the roof – an die Decke gehen; to bark – schnauzen;
curt – schroff

Thank heavens for that, I thought. At least I can go to the fashion show this afternoon.

But Mum was of a different opinion. "You don't actually think I'm going to let you go after what you've done?"

"But Mum," I protested. "It was all so harmless."

"You call that harmless? Being taken to the police station like some **tart**?"

"But there were loads of girls my age in the disco. They weren't tarts. I mean, they didn't check our **ID** at the entrance, they just let us in. We thought it couldn't be that bad ..." I tried to take the blame off my shoulders and share it with a few others.

"I don't care what you think. The fact is you should know what's **appropriate** for your age and what's not. Midnight visits to the disco are definitely *out*!"

I gave in, **overcome with remorse**. Showing as much remorse as possible was my only hope. I just had to go to the fashion show, whatever it took. Not only was it the last show, the winners would be announced afterwards. But even more important was the fact that I just had to ask Percy if he wanted to go out with me or Mona.

But Mum remained **merciless**.

"This conversation is over," she said in the end impatiently. "You're not going, and that's that."

"You – you can't do this to me!" I cried angrily and **on the brink of tears**. "You don't know what you're doing! You – you're ruining my chance of happiness!"

---

tart – Schlampe; ID – Ausweis; appropriate – angemessen; overcome with remorse – zerknirscht; merciless – unerbittlich; on the brink of tears – den Tränen nahe

Then I really did break down into tears. I rushed out of the kitchen, **slammed** the door behind me, and disappeared into my room.

The telephone rang. Franzi. Of course, she'd read the newspaper. But instead of feeling sorry for me, she was the personification of sensationalism. Only once I'd told her everything, right down to the smallest detail, did she have an ear for the tragic situation I was now in.

"You have to find **allies**," she suggested at the end of our conversation. "People who can convince your mother that the show can't **take place** without you."

I'd only just hung up when the phone rang again.

I almost dropped the **receiver** in surprise. It was Mona.

"Have your parents said you can't go to the fashion show as well?" she asked without beating about the bush.

She had, in fact, already called Mrs Berger and told her about the situation.

"So, listen," she said, "Berger said she would get onto the Centre-Manager so that he can **work on** our parents."

"Great," I said, feeling really relieved. "So there's a **glimmer of hope**."

I called Debbie. Her parents had reacted just like Mona's mum and mine. So I quickly told her the good news, but she said, "The Centre-Manager will have to use all his **powers of persuasion** to talk my dad round – or he could just give him two **cartons** of cigarettes."

---

to slam – knallen; ally – Verbündete; to take place – stattfinden;
receiver – Hörer; to work on – bearbeiten;
glimmer of hope – Hoffnungsschimmer;
powers of persuasion – Überredungskünste; carton – Stange

As it turned out, both methods had to be called upon – the art of persuasion and **bribery**.

Mum said, "OK, OK. I'll let you go, even if it does go against my principles. Your father won't speak to me for a week, but it's better than completely ruining the fashion show. I didn't know you had such a crucial role."

I only **inadvertently** found out later that the Centre-Manager had managed to persuade my mum with the promise of a little contract.

I can't describe how hectic things were.

Everyone was getting ready for the big goodbye. There was **wistfulness** in the air. People kept hugging each other and saying how sad they were that everything was over already. At the same time the **stress levels** were really rising. People kept complaining about one thing or the other. I felt really sorry for the hairdressers and make-up artists. Even Ken was treated like a dogsbody by quite a few girls. The poor guy was constantly sent off to look for things that had gone missing – lipstick, mascara, tights and even for **bras**! Miss Dreary-Face had **mislaid** her horrible shiny green handbag for the third set, and Verena accused me of stealing her hairpin! Even Debbie – who was normally a picture of **stoical** calmness and anything but bitchy – **bawled** at a girl from her group because she'd just caught her putting on her tights.

---

bribery – Bestechung; inadvertently – zufällig;
wistfulness – Wehmut; stress levels – Stresspegel;
bra – Büstenhalter; to mislay sth – etwas verlegen;
stoical – stoisch; to bawl – brüllen

"But mine had a **ladder** in them," said the girl as Debbie forced her to take off her tights.

The **impending** announcement of the competition winners was clearly putting everybody on edge. Even Shalima and Mrs Berger seemed to be nervous. Shalima kept running around with her notepad. She seemed to be busy **adding up** the points for the competition.

"It's all just show," said Ali with a grin as he sorted out the CDs on his sampler for the last time. "They've known the winner **for ages**."

"Really?" I asked, astonished. "You mean, there are no more points today?"

"Points?" Ali grinned even more. "Come on, girl, you don't actually believe all that **claptrap**, do you?! Mrs Berger and Shalima picked the winner on the first day. They can tell who'll make it in the fashion business and who's right for their agency at first sight."

I was utterly flabbergasted. That couldn't be true! And I'd been giving my best for each single point the whole time! Points for performance, points for looking after my clothes, points for being **cooperative** ... Was that all just a facade? Didn't it have any influence on the decision?

"You're **pulling my leg**," I muttered, **distraught**.

Ali looked at me full of pity. "You're almost as naïve as you are good-looking," he said. "The modelling business

---

ladder – Laufmasche; impending – bevorstehend;
to add up – addieren; for ages – schon lange;
claptrap – Geschwätz; cooperative – kollegial;
to pull sb's leg – jmdn. auf den Arm nehmen;
distraught – verstört

is really tough. It's not all just about looking good. You know what the most important thing is? **Usability**."

"And what does that mean?" I asked **inquisitively**. I really had no idea what he was talking about.

But, unfortunately, Shalima pushed her way between us before Ali could answer. "Why are you standing around backstage? You're not even changed yet. Come on, off to the changing room with you!"

Despite being nervous, everybody put on a really good last show.

In the middle of doing the last set with Mona and the boys, I suddenly felt really sad that everything was over. I couldn't imagine what my life would be like without the fashion show – without the chic clothes, without the make-up artist and hairdresser, without the music, and above all, without Percy.

*Don't wait for the future because it's right under your nose. Today is everything* ... I had to hold onto him. If all my catwalk dreams were to be over, I had to at least save him. He could become a part of my boring teenage life!

The big finale was about to start. We presented party clothes, conjuring up a **hint** of Milan and Paris on the catwalk, while performing a choreography to the Gerri Halliwell hit, *It's raining men*.

I was feeling really upbeat as Percy suddenly whispered something into my ear before making our entrance. "You've never looked as beautiful as you do today."

---

usability – Verwertbarkeit; inquisitively – wissbegierig;
hint – Hauch

I felt myself go red. The rouge which the make-up artist had so carefully dabbed onto my **cheekbones** was superfluous again. He really was a sweet-talker!

With a sudden **surge** of my sense of reality I asked, "Have you already said that to Mona?"

He looked at me strangely for a moment. Then he gave me a cheeky grin and said, "No, but thanks for reminding me."

And then he just **slipped** through my fingers. Just you wait, I thought. You won't be able to get away. After the show your time will come!

I enjoyed my last performance on the catwalk, and I was really pleased to see Franzi and the *Pepper Dollies* amongst the audience. Mum was standing in the gallery on the first floor with people from her agency and the Joker and – I couldn't believe my eyes – Dad was standing next to her.

That can't be true! Why didn't he drag me off the catwalk personally? Someone must have **cast a spell** on him!

After the finale Mrs Berger, who was **dressed to kill** as ever, took the microphone to announce the winner of the modelling competition. All the girls were about to explode with nervousness.

We all expected Percy to win in the boys' section, and so it came as no surprise when she **declared** him the winner and put a golden **sash** around his neck.

---

cheekbones – Wangenknochen; surge – Aufwallen;
to slip – flutschen; to cast a spell – verhexen;
dressed to kill – todschick; to declare – verkünden; sash – Schärpe

That was the start of his career, I thought to myself, and deep down I really hoped that I would be the winner of the girls' category – me and not Mona – so that I could go with him. We were such a beautiful couple – and definitely "**usable**"!

"It was much more difficult to reach a decision for the girls," Mrs Berger started the **lead-up** to announcing the female winner. "They all performed exceptionally well, and they proved themselves to be extremely cooperative. Each girl is as pretty as the next. That, dear audience, is something you've just seen for yourselves. So I'd like to ask you to give our non-professional models a really big round of applause. If I could introduce them to you individually …"

She waved us to the front. "You saw … Verena, Debbie, May, Cindy, Mona and Kiki."

Was I being **oversensitive** or did the applause just get louder as Mona and I came onto the catwalk? Why was my name called last? Did that mean I'd made it into the last round? Had I perhaps …? My knees were trembling with excitement. Could my dream actually come true?

We were soon all standing at the T-end of the catwalk, staring tensely at Mrs Berger. The Centre-Manager had also come onto the catwalk.

Mrs Berger went up to him and handed him an envelope. He tore it open, looked at the contents for a moment with an expression of slight surprise and then took up the microphone.

---

usable – verwertbar; lead-up – Einleitung;
oversensitive – überempfindlich

"I don't want to **keep** you all **on tenterhooks** any longer. The winner of our competition and the City-Centre model is …"

Then he made a really long dramatic pause. Come on, I thought, tell me before I have a heart attack!

"Yes, ladies and gentlemen, the City-Centre model of the year is … our **enchanting** Miss-Morning-Queen, the Face of the Month, our very own Cindy!"

The blood just rushed from my face. I almost **fainted**.

That dreary-faced cow? What did she have that I didn't?

"**As opposed to** you she has contacts to television and teeny-magazines. That's very **handy** for the agency," explained Ali as he **dismantled** his **gear**. "Like I said, being beautiful is good, but usability is better!"

I was feeling completely frustrated because I hadn't won a single prize. And yet so many people had tipped me to win the main prize! The only thing I could take with me was a red rose which the Centre-Manager had pressed into my hand with a dry kiss on my cheek like all the other participants. And, of course, a lot of experience.

After the local photographers tried to blind us all in a frenzy of flashing cameras, it was finally time to say goodbye backstage with some **sparkling wine** and soda and a few **titbits**.

---

to keep sb on tenterhooks – jmdn. auf die Folter spannen; enchanting – bezaubernd; to faint – ohnmächtig werden; as opposed to – im Gegensatz zu; handy – nützlich; to dismantle – demontieren; gear – Ausrüstung; sparkling wine – Sekt; titbit – Leckerbissen

Franzi and the *Pepper Dollies* had somehow managed to **fudge** their way through the barrier and they paid me a quick visit to **console** me.

"It was definitely **rigged**," complained Franzi irately, and Lea said, "Really, you should have won! You were probably just too young."

Even the Joker and Dad did their best to comfort me, though Dad couldn't help saying, "I hope this was a **salutary** experience which has **cured** you once and for all of this modelling nonsense."

Mum, however, was really angry. "They said every participant would receive a voucher," she grumbled. "It's nothing but **exploitation**! How much money do you think it would have cost if they'd have had professional models here! It's really **stingy**!" And she set off to find the Centre-Manager and get our vouchers for us.

Yes, and then it really was all over. I gave Debbie a goodbye kiss and she almost burst into tears. We **swore** to each other **blindly** that we wouldn't lose contact again.

"Come on, Kiki," said Mona to me shortly afterwards. "We have to **take** Percy **to task** now. It's high time!" She hadn't won anything either and was just as disappointed as I was – which didn't seem to have any effect on her thirst for action.

---

to fudge – mogeln; to console – trösten; rigged – manipuliert;
salutary – heilsam; to cure – heilen; exploitation – Ausbeutung;
stingy – knauserig;
to swear blindly – hoch und heilig versprechen;
to take sb to task – jmdn. zur Rede stellen

So I grabbed a full glass of sparkling wine and followed Mona to look for Percy.

In the end, we found him near one of the big columns in a somewhat unusual position.

"What's he doing there?" I asked, slightly puzzled.

Mona swallowed. "I'd say he was snogging with someone."

"I beg your pardon?" I couldn't believe what I was hearing. "I want to see that for myself," I said and hurried over to the column **with fierce determination** in order to get to the bottom of it.

The sparkling wine which I'd brought for Percy **sloshed** out of the glass. What I then saw, made me scream with horror and drop my glass.

Percy in an intimate embrace with … Cindy, the dreariest face in the world!

As the glass **shattered** on the floor, the two of them stopped snogging and turned to us.

I stared at the **entangled** couple in bewilderment, then at Mona. The look in her eyes **spoke volumes** as well. The answer we were looking for was standing in front of us. There was no need to bother running after this **two-faced** Casanova anymore!

"Well, you certainly didn't hang around long!" Mona couldn't help saying.

And I added in disgust, "Playing us off against each

---

with fierce determination – wild entschlossen;
to slosh – schwappen; to shatter – zerbrechen;
entangled – umschlungen; to speak volumes – Bände sprechen;
two-faced – heuchlerisch

other and then running off with her! How long have you known that she was going to win? Right from the first day? Unfortunately, I can't compete with her connections, you're right there!"

I grabbed Mona's hand and pulled her away before Percy could say anything.

But Cindy called after us, of course. "It's not my fault you're such bad losers!"

We went into the changing room feeling completely frustrated and picked up our things.

"That **rogue**!" Mona cursed to herself. "He was sweet-talking me and then he goes off with that bird."

I could well understand her **exasperation**.

"Let's go and have a coffee," I suggested because I had to calm down, too. First we really let off steam and then we decided to finally bury the hatchet between us.

"And what shall we do now?" I asked. "We can't just let him get away with it. He played us off from the very beginning – probably just to help Cindy out. I bet it was all just a **put-up job**!"

Mona thought the same. I could see that she was already **wracking her brains** to think of a way to get her **revenge** on Percy.

"Listen," she said in the end. "I've got an idea how to give him a good dressing-down!" She lent over the table to me and whispered something in my ear.

---

rogue – Schuft; exasperation – Verärgerung;
a put-up job – eine abgekartete Sache;
to wrack one's brains – sich das Hirn zermartern;
revenge – Rache

"Wicked!" I cried with a giggle. "That's just so nasty! We have to do it!"

We **sealed** our new alliance with a handshake and decided to call the revenge-is-sweet hotline at the local radio station the next day and kiss goodbye to Percy! No girl around here would ever fall for his tricks again.

I was just about to leave the City-Centre and go over to Mum's agency so she could take me home, when my mobile peeped and I got an SMS.

*You should have won today,* I read. *I thought you were the most beautiful of them all. ILU2bits Meik.*

So he'd been there and had seen me in the last show. Me and Mona! But he'd sent *me* a SMS. That could only mean ...

*Where are you?* I texted back.

*At the Gertrude fountain. Fancy letting off some steam with me?*

I grinned. There he was again! But perhaps it wasn't such a bad idea. I went over to the fountain which was really nearby.

"Let's go to the gravel pit," suggested Meik. "It's going to be **sunset** soon."

Shortly afterwards I was sitting at the gravel pit with Meik. No one said a word, and we just stared at the gently **rippling** water. The sun slowly turned into a circle of orange and red. Hadn't we been in this situation before? Whatever! This time things were different. My mind was

---

to seal – besiegeln; sunset – Sonnenuntergang;
to ripple – kräuseln

free of the Percys and Monas of this world. I was completely in the Here and Now, and that was Meik only. Sweet, dear, **reliable** Meik.

I hadn't got over the disappointment at how the modelling competition ended. I was still feeling really frustrated and **used**. But I still had the feeling I would really like to have started a modelling career!

As if Meik had read my thoughts, he suddenly said: "You're really good-looking, but I still think it wouldn't be a good idea for you to model."

"Why not?" I asked. "Because you're so jealous?"

He laughed. "Any boy would be jealous if he had such a pretty girlfriend and other boys kept smiling at her on the catwalk."

Oh no, not that again!

He shook his head. "No, that's not the reason. I just think you can lose your sense of reality really quickly in a scene like that. What do you think?"

I had to admit he was right.

"I can imagine it's more and more difficult in a business like that to recognise what's really important in life as time goes on," he continued.

"And what is important?" I asked with interest.

"You," he said resolutely and without the slightest hesitation. "You as a person, not as a fashion doll!"

Then he fell silent and looked out over the sunset. He ran his hand through his blond hair. "You just don't fit there. You're not a doll, you're far too impulsive, too … lively. That's why you couldn't win. You don't fit the

---

reliable – verlässlich; used – ausgebeutet

mould.“ He **caressed** my cheek. ″What do you need a spotlight for?“ he said. ″Your face is much more beautiful now, lit by the evening sun.“

I sighed, no boy had ever said anything like that to me before, and it sounded so much more honest than Percy's sweet-talking.

″You're so romantic,“ I said full of wonder.

He grinned. ″Is that a problem?“

Blimey, no way! I thought it was marvellous, and so I said, ″No, it's just right!“

When he kissed me, I didn't have the feeling that we had to practise anymore. All of a sudden, he was no longer a stranger to me. I felt closer to him than any other person.

Something cheered for joy in me and wanted to hold onto him forever – as tight as I could – and never let go.

That must be love.

**The End**

---

to caress – streicheln

Ebenfalls auf Englisch bei Thienemann erschienen:

Sabine Both: *Move to Cloud Nine*
Brinx/Kömmerling: *A Paul to Kiss*
Christamaria Fiedler: *Spaghetti Crime*
Sissi Flegel: *Forbidden to Love*
Bianka Minte-König: *Mobile Phone Love*
Hortense Ullrich: *Never Kiss a Witch,*
*Love is Blonde*
Zimmermann & Zimmermann:
*Maths, Stress and a Lovesick Heart*
*Summer, Sun & Holiday Love*

Falls du Lust hast, Bianka Minte-König eine Mail
zu schicken, hier die Adresse:
autorin@biankaminte-koenig.de

**Minte-König, Bianka:**
Schoolyard Flirt & Catwalk Dreams
Aus dem Deutschen von David Fermer
ISBN 13: 978 3 522 17806 8
ISBN 10: 3 522 17806 8

Reihengestaltung: Birgit Schössow
Einbandillustration: Birgit Schössow
Schrift: Aldus Roman und Handwriting
Satz: KCS GmbH, Buchholz/Hamburg
Reproduktion: Medienfabrik, Möglingen
Druck und Bindung: Friedrich Pustet, Regensburg

5 4 3 2 1* 06 07 08 09

www.thienemann.de
www.frechemaedchen.de
www.biankaminte-koenig.de